# DOWN COBBLED STREETS

*In memory of my parents who ensured for us a secure childhood, and for Anne who unexpectedly died as this book was being written.*

# DOWN
## COBBLED
# STREETS

A
LIBERTIES
CHILDHOOD

PHIL
O'KEEFFE

First published in 1995 by
Brandon Book Publishers Ltd
Dingle, Co. Kerry, Ireland

British Library Cataloguing in Publication Data is available for this book.

10 9 8 7 6 5 4 3

ISBN 0 86322 213 7

Cover photograph by Nevill Johnson
reproduced by kind permission of Radio Teilifís Éireann
Cover designed by The Public Communications Centre Ltd, Dublin
Printed by ColourBooks Ltd, Dublin

# Contents

Another Little Girl     7

Walking the Slang Wall     22

The Keys Around My Neck     32

Walking Taller     49

Our Daily Bread     64

Tobacco, Snuff and Chalk     78

She's Not Dawney     96

The Busiest Day of the Week     113

Sunday     126

Spring Cleaning     145

A Letter from the Country     153

Marble Red, Marble Blue     171

War Clouds Over Dublin     184

A Little Learning     199

Breaking the Mould     215

With this pen I have cut the cord
Which bound me to you
From the day of my birth.
With these words I have exorcised
The spirit within
Which has haunted and teased me.
I am free.

*Phil O'Keeffe*

# Another Little Girl

I was a light sleeper and sounds in the night disturbed me easily. In the early morning darkness, the low murmur of my mother's voice in the room across the landing wakened me. I raised myself on my elbow and listened. Babs, my older sister by four years, with whom I shared a double bed, ignored my efforts to waken her and pulled the bedclothes closer around her head.

I cocked my ears to the sounds coming from my parents' bedroom. I heard their door open and my father begin to tiptoe down the stairs in his stockinged feet. I gathered my thin nightdress about me, put my bare feet on the cold linoleum floor and crept out to the landing. Three steps to the corner of the stairs and I could see my father by the front door, slipping on his shoes and reaching for his jacket. He glanced up and saw me at the head of the stairs.

"It's all right," he said. There was a gentle knock on the door and he turned to open it.

"I saw the light in the front room," a voice said.

"She's started," I heard him say. "I was just going for Nanny." He came to the foot of the stairs.

"Go back to bed, like a good little girl," he said. "I won't be long, child, and here's somebody to look after you."

Mrs Tierney, Jennie's mother, closed the door quietly after my father. What was ailing Mother, I wondered, if my father was hurrying for Nanny at this hour of the morning? It was grey and misty outside, and a good mile and a half to Nanny's house in South Earl Street. My father's hurrying added to my unease. I never liked to see men hurrying. They never seemed able to settle for a good run, but huffled and shuffled and blew their breaths out in short gasps, especially when the factory horns were sounding their last warning at eight o'clock in the morning. Women took hurrying in their stride, pushing prams and go-cars speedily up and down paths, but when a man moved fast something was wrong.

My mother, who was an only child, depended on her cousins for help in times of sickness. She had many relatives on her mother's side, and Nanny was the one we knew best. My mother's first cousin and her senior by some ten years, she called to our house frequently. She rarely troubled the front door. She would come silently through the back gate, along the garden path, quietly lift the latch on the kitchen door and whisper, "It's only me." Then she would settle herself without ceremony at the kitchen table and announce:

"I'm not stoppin'. I've only got a minute."

"Open your coat, Nanny, and take off your hat," my mother would say, placing a mug of tea in front of her.

"I'm not stoppin', Peg. I have to see to Johnny's tea. And I'll not open me coat, I've only me old bib on." And though her quick visit might last for several hours, her coat would remain firmly buttoned and her hat stay anchored to her head with two enormous hat-pins.

One by one we had made our way down to the kitchen where Jennie's mother was rattling mugs and plates and buttering slices of bread. Madge, the eldest of us children, took her mothering duties very seriously and ordered the rest of us to sit quietly on the wooden form in the corner of the kitchen while she helped Mrs Tierney prepare breakfast. Babs and I were left to dress Betty who was four-and-a-bit and Tess who was only three, pushing them into vests and bodices and mixing up their dresses and pinnies with all our effort. We shushed them vigorously as we bent and stretched and crooked their arms into their clothes.

Nanny arrived ahead of my father's return.

"You're all good childer, every one of ye," she said as she patted each of our heads in turn. "Just shish now, not a word, while I go and see to your mother."

At the door to the parlour she said to Mrs Tierney, "Is she far gone, d'ye know?"

"Fairly on, she thinks herself."

"I sent Joe to leave word with Mrs Duffy – she shouldn't be long. This one might be quick."

"You go up and see to her; I'll stay down here with these."

My father came back close on Nanny's heels and relieved Jennie's mother of our care.

"I'll go," she said. "I'm beyond if ye need me." She closed the front door behind her and went back to getting her own four children ready for the day.

"Can I have a cut of bread and jam?" I asked. Hunger was beginning to take over from uncertainty and, besides, Father was back to look after us. Nanny passed through with a cup of tea for my mother, so I felt things were beginning to be a bit more normal. As it was only eight o'clock in the morning and much too early to go anywhere, we collected our slices of bread and jam and mugs of milky tea and sat quietly listening to the noises from upstairs.

Nanny appeared at the table. Her hat was still fixed to her head, but the coat was gone and she wore a blue cross-over bib, neatly tied at the back. "Your mother wants to see ye before ye go to school."

None of us rushed to be first up the stairs. Nanny took Betty and Tess by the hand and pushed Madge, Babs and me ahead of her. My mother's bedroom door was open, but we halted on the threshold. I balanced the ball of my foot on the saddle of the door and looked into the room. The sun crept in under the fringe of the holland blind and slanted to the end of the little gas-fire, brightening the dull whiteness of the jagged fire-clay sticks through which the gas-jet flamed and glinting on the flat metal starter at the side. There was no roar and hiss from the fire today.

"Don't stand there, children. Let me see ye." We inched inside the door, Nanny holding Tess in her arms and restraining Betty who wanted to climb onto my mother's bed. She lay in semi-darkness in the big double bed tucked into the corner of the room. In the other corner a small table stood under the red glow of the tin Sacred Heart lamp. There was a big roll of cotton wool, with its dark blue wrapping opened, and a lot of what looked like folded blay calico sheets and a towel on the table. My mother caught my glance and I saw her nod to Nanny. To Madge she said, "Take Tess with ye to school today. Sister Magdalen won't mind. Just tell her I'm not well."

I wanted to ask her why she wasn't well, but some instinct held me back. She had been all right the night before. She had been tired and gone to bed early, but she had taken to resting lately, so I saw nothing wrong with that. Now she appealed to Babs and me, "You'll help, won't ye," she said, "and keep out of Daddy's and Nanny's way?"

We nodded solemnly. I wondered why Mother didn't raise herself in the bed. She lay with her hair brushed back from her forehead and her face was unusually pale. I was frightened, and I knew my sisters were, too. We turned gratefully when a knock on the front door sounded. We smiled tentatively at our mother, and as I turned to crowd past Nanny I glanced at the picture of Our Lady which hung over the Sacred Heart lamp; her gaze seemed to follow me out of the room.

My father had the door-catch in his hand as we trooped down the stairs and he shooed us past him into the parlour. We stood there, a silent group, while he opened the front door. A little figure holding a big bag stood outside. She bobbed her head to my father.

"Upstairs," he said, and no other word passed between them. Silently she climbed the stairs, a black cloak held tightly about her, her neat buttoned boots hardly making a sound.

"Who's that?" I whispered to Madge.

"It's Mrs Duffy," she whispered back.

"Who's Mrs Duffy?" I asked slowly, but Madge was leading the way into the kitchen where she fussed about, instructing us to put pinnies on over our dresses and to finish our bread and jam. My father closed the front door and followed into the kitchen.

"Has Mrs Duffy got a new baby in her black bag?" I asked. My two older sisters whirled round and stared at me.

"Stop moiderin' me and eat your breakfast," my father commanded, making a bee-line for the scullery to hide his confusion. But I liked to have my questions answered and I persisted.

"Has she brought Mam a new baby?" I trailed after him.

"Who put such silly ideas into your head? Go out and play in the yard until it's time for school."

You didn't persist with questions when Father used that tone of voice.

"You'll take Tess to school with ye today," he said. Relieved of his responsibilities once he had fetched Nanny and Mrs

Duffy, he didn't want any little ones under his feet. "She'd only be in the way," he said. In the way of what? I wanted to ask, but bit back the words. "The nuns won't mind ye keepin' Tess in the class with ye." The nuns never minded. They were used to very young children being brought into school when a mother was unwell or had to attend the hospital, and we were used to having little sisters and brothers squeezed into our desks. But this was the first time it had happened to us. My mother had never been ill before.

Father helped us get our lunches ready and we started for school earlier than normal so that we could wait for Sister Magdalen, the head nun, outside her office. Tess we carried between us, linking our arms to make a carry-chair down the long haul of Cork Street and up Ormond Street until we reached the school gate.

When school was over that day we made the long journey home, slower this time because we were tired and Tess and Betty wanted to sleep. The excitement of the morning had faded with the matter-of-factness of school, but when we saw Father at the dinner-table, ladling mashed potatoes into great hills on our plates, we felt very uneasy.

"Is Mrs Duffy still here?" I had noticed a glass rimmed with dregs of porter on the draining-board.

"She is," my father answered, without looking up.

"And Nanny, where is she?"

"Upstairs." Turning to Madge he said, "When the dinner's finished, take them down to Mrs Tierney. You can play there till it's time to scald the tea. Don't any of ye come trottin' back until ye're called."

No Mam at the dinner-table or to tell us to take off our school dresses and put on our old clothes. We put the pinnies on again and scattered out to play. Mrs Tierney lived four houses down from us. She and her husband were good neighbours to my parents and they to them. She was Jennie's mother and Jennie was my best friend. There were six months between us in age, but Jennie came second in her family, and like me she didn't carry the responsibility loaded on the shoulders of an eldest child.

She was shoulder-high to my tallness, with soft chubby cheeks. I always thought she looked like a russet-red apple, and I envied her her nicely rounded arms which turned a smooth dark brown in summer, when I kept my skinny arms covered up. Her hair was short and dark and framed two nearly black brown eyes which now stared soberly at me.

"How do you know she brings a baby in her bag?"

I had told her about Mrs Duffy and what had happened that morning. There were already two younger children in Jennie's family, just like mine, and she had accepted each baby's arrival without comment, but she was prepared to allow that maybe, just maybe, I might be right.

"You know, when we got our last baby," she said, "well it wasn't your Mrs Duffy who brought it. It was a black doctor on a bicycle." Then she looked at me again. "Hey," she said, "he had a bag too!"

"Let's play near the end of the hill," I said. "We'll make beds and we'll be able to see when Mrs Duffy goes past."

Our house was one of four which stood on a slight incline, our hill, a little apart from the other houses. Jennie had chalk in her schoolbag and between us we marked out our pickie beds. We drew a large oblong and divided it into smaller sections of numbered squares, diamond quarters, a narrow oblong which was called "skinny-eight", and two further squares. The sections were numbered from one to ten and the game was to kick a pickie, a shoe-polish tin filled with sand, and shiny and skiddy from much sliding, into the various sections, one number after the other, without the pickie or the player landing on any of the chalked lines. If this happened you forfeited your chance and had to start again after everybody else had had their go.

I was negotiating the problem of hopping on one leg and kicking the pickie into the skinny-eight, when Jennie hissed at me, "She's coming." I yelped and spread my arms wide in an attempt to retain my balance, but I fell over and was ruled out. I looked up to see our front gate open and close. We drew back to let Mrs Duffy pass. She looked like the witches in our story books, though she didn't have a pointed hat like they had: she had a crinkled bonnet with wispy bits of grey hair peeping out under each side. She wore a black cloak which fell from her shoulders, making her look very tiny. We could see the side of the mysterious black bag which she carried close to her. She didn't even glance in our direction as she passed by and continued down our road with her little bird-like steps.

I abandoned Jennie and the pickie-beds and ran as fast as I could across the empty space at the back of our house and threw myself at the scullery door. Nanny was in the kitchen drinking a mug of tea.

"Did ye come to see the new baby, child?" she said as I skidded to a halt. I stared at her.

"New baby?" I echoed.

Nanny sat with her two elbows on the table and the mug cupped in her hands. Her steady gaze stopped my questions tumbling out.

"Hush now," she said as she stood up to lower the gas under the big pot of boiling water. She patted me on the shoulder. "You're a canny one," she said. "I told your father you'd been in this world before. Anyway, you're the first to know – the others are not in yet."

"What is it?" I said as I turned to follow her.

"A child," she said, "another little girl, God bless and preserve her. The seventh little girl and born with a caul – a lucky one that, and a lovely little baby." She paused as she turned back to the table.

"Child," she said, "don't be at your father at a time like this. Like as not, he'll lose his rag with ye."

Another little girl: we were six now. We would have been seven, but a baby sister of fourteen months, beloved and beautiful, had died, just before I was born.

"The doctor from the Coombe will be here shortly," Father told us as we helped him set the table for the tea. "Before he comes I think ye should go to see the new baby."

"Remember, your mother needs her rest," Nanny cautioned as we trooped upstairs.

Mother lay on her side, protecting a little bundle which lay beside her. As we tip-toed into the room she held her fingers to her lips and beckoned us forward. Madge lifted Betty and Tess in turn to look at the tiny bundle.

"Isn't she beautiful?" my mother whispered. "Do you like her?"

The baby's face peeped out of the wrapping which co-cooned her little body. We reached out our hands to touch her, and Nanny stood guard so that we didn't touch what she called "the soft spot" on top of her head. The baby stirred and we quickly withdrew, anxious not to waken her further.

Mother was not allowed out of bed for the nine days of her confinement, but it was understood that Nanny would stay until she was relieved by another of our cousins. Nanny believed in taking life easy and nothing ever seemed to trouble her, not even the thought of her own husband and brood whom she hadn't seen since early morning and might not see now until the following day. She was a generous and loving person and did not mind all the slopping and possing out of baby cloths which seemed to be inevitable after the birth of a baby. Already baby cloths flapped on the line and hung on the wooden clothes horse beside the kitchen range.

My father's job now was to look after us five girls and entertain any callers and visitors.

"She did bring it in her black bag, didn't she?" Father, standing in the middle of the kitchen, looked startled.

"You said the doctor from the Coombe was coming. Is the baby sick?"

"You're a right heart-scald with your questions. I need more cheese for the sandwiches." My father pushed the money at me. "Go to the Deerpark dairy and ask her to slice you a half-pound of cheese. And don't delay – I want you back here." As I opened the door to the back garden, I saw Nanny lift her head from possing out and nod slowly to my father.

"I told ye, Joe," she said, "that one sees and hears too much."

The doctor from the Coombe was just leaving when I arrived back from the shop. Taking his bicycle from where he had propped it by the gate, he stood talking to my father for a few moments. I stared at him. He was black. The doctors who sat in the dispensary or came to the school to give us a check-up, or even the doctors in the hospitals, all had the same pinky-yellow skin that we had. We didn't see many black people around our way, and to my mind that made him very important.

The rest of that evening and the following days were taken up by a constant stream of visitors. Besides Jennie's mother and father, my parents had few close friends in the immediate neighbourhood, but babies were God's blessing on a family and so there were many gentle taps on the door. In whispered conversations everybody was told that mother and baby were resting. At a time like this neighbours would never intrude nor come beyond the doorstep even if invited to do so: they just wanted to know that the mother was well, and then they smiled and were gone. The real visitors were my mother's cousins: it was the women who called. There were some we called "Aunt" and more were referred to as "Mrs", and it did not always do to step over the boundary between the two. The aunts could look after themselves if needs be and could be depended upon to wash the teacups; the other cousins were offered a glass of sherry or port and somebody sat dutifully beside them to keep them company. Most of the time we were shooed out to play, but when we dashed in from the back and were brought face to face with the women in the parlour, we came under close scrutiny.

"And what book are you in now?"

I would have liked to say that they didn't put us in books in school; that I was in First Class, thank you, and no, I didn't need somebody to put a weight on my head because I was growing so tall. But I was in enough trouble already, and giving cheeky answers to our cousins would have been the last straw, so I said nothing.

My mother looked better each morning, though she was still not allowed to do anything. The baby lay in a wooden cot most of the time between feedings, and for the first few days was given sugar and water from a flat-bottomed feeding bottle shaped a little like a boat, with a big brown sucker at one end.

"Has your baby been christened yet?" Joan, Maddy, Jennie and I were sitting on some blocks in our back yard. We were preparing for a game of shop and had gathered old bits of delph, china and glass to stock the shelves.

"If she dies without being baptised, she'll go to limbo."

"She's not going to die!" I was horrified at the thought, and suspended my smashing of the china, which we were crushing into fragments to resemble different kinds of sweets. Who wanted to make chaneys when the issue of whether my baby sister was about to die or not was in question? "Who says she's going to die?"

"My mam says ye never know with babies nowadays," Ann nodded wisely like an old granny, while busily knocking lumps out of a piece of green glass with a sharp stone. "They can be snuffed out quickly – so my mam says," she added hastily.

"If she's not baptised in time then her soul won't be cleansed of original sin and she has to stay in limbo. That's what the catechism says," Joan added, sorting the chaneys into little piles.

"And she'll stay there until the Day of Final Judgement, which means that if she dies now without baptism and then you die and go straight to purgatory or heaven, you won't see her ever again until after the Last Day."

We all sat back, considering the prospect. The chaneys and the shop weren't important anymore. In some way the threat of limbo was even more frightening than death. But I needn't have worried. My mother and those around her knew the danger of sudden illness and infant deaths, and had no intention of delaying the ceremony.

"Would you like to see her christened?"

I didn't know why I was singled out, but my mother did not have to ask a second time. She herself would not attend the christening, which was done while she was still confined to bed. A grandmother usually carried the infant to the church, but both our grandmothers were either in purgatory or heaven, so Nanny stepped into the breach again. A cousin of my mother's, Julia, would act as godmother. On the third day after her birth our little baby sister, who was to be called Nance, was dressed in the family christening robe of white satin, with ribbons and deep lace at the hem and sleeves, and a white satin-quilted bonnet. A small christening veil was placed over her and would remain there until the priest lifted it to pronounce the words of baptism. My mother withdrew from its bed of blue paper a large white shawl which she had crocheted, and which had been used for each of our baptisms, and wrapped it round the baby.

The mile-and-a-half walk to the church in Donore Avenue was pleasant, particularly as I had the day off school. My father did not attend, and we had no godfather. Births, christenings and churchings were the responsibility of women; men could not take precious time off work.

There were other babies for christening that day and ours squealed with the rest of them when the cold water of baptism was poured on her head.

"A lucky sign when she cries," Nanny explained as we sat by the side of the christening font, while I prayed that the spluttering and choking I heard didn't mean that my little sister was about to die.

We had a slow journey home as neighbours and sometimes total strangers asked to see the baby. They wouldn't have dared to stop us on the way to the church, but now that she was baptised they could lift the veil and look at her lovely face.

"She's the livin' image of her father."

"She's the dead spit of her mother."

"Indeed she's not, she's the image of herself, aren't ye, pet?"

I agreed with Nanny. The baby looked like a baby, and anybody who said otherwise needed to have their eyes examined. She was a strong baby, too, and was bawling her head off. My worries about limbo faded into the background.

"Would you like to go with Julia?" my mother asked when we arrived home. "You know the people better than she does." Visiting the neighbours with the newly christened child was an old Dublin custom which my mother could not ignore. If she did, she knew she would be charged with being uppity.

"Does she think she's a cut above the rest of us?"

My mother did not believe she was a cut above anybody, but she did have a natural reserve and tended to keep herself to herself. She gave me strict instructions as to who we should visit and who we should not. There were some whose pride would be sorely hurt if we didn't visit, even though it would cost them money they could ill afford. Silver coins, from a half-crown to a threepenny piece, were pressed into the tiny infant hand and skilfully removed by Julia. My mother agonised over this; she knew in her heart that the ones who could least afford it would make the biggest gesture.

It was toward the end of Mother's nine compulsory days in bed that Lily, my godmother, arrived to walk her to the chapel in Donore Avenue.

"It's time to get churched, Peg," she said.

Until she was properly churched she should not go to Mass or Holy Communion, cook food or leave the house to do her shopping.

"Not until she finishes this," my father insisted, pouring porter into a glass. "It gets harder and harder to make her take it."

"Ye'll have to try, Peg," said Lily, adding her persuasion to my father's. "It's the best tonic you can get, and you know it."

My father added milk to the porter, making a dirty brown liquid with no froth on top. I did not blame my mother for not wanting to drink it, but it was recommended by the doctor, my grandfather who worked in Guinness's Brewery, and all her cousins, so I supposed it must have something in its favour.

"What is churching?" I ventured to ask my father, but he didn't know. My mother, when I asked her, knew it was a blessing at the altar and it was given to mothers after their babies were born. I didn't dare ask the nuns in school. You didn't raise that sort of thing with them, about babies and where they came from and why my mother had to be churched, but the next time the priest came to the school I decided to risk it. There was a long pause while he looked at me, and then across to the nun at the head of the class.

"Churching, well, let's see. Churching is... well, shall we say, churching is a prayer of the church for cleansing. Do you understand cleansing? Does she understand cleansing, Sister?"

"Yes, Father," I said before Sister could say anything.

"How old are you?" he said.

"Six – just seven, Father."

"You'll be making your Holy Communion shortly?"

"Next May, Father."

"Well, you're too young to be bothering your head with such things. Go out and play when you get home, like a good child, and help your mother all you can."

Obediently I said, "Yes, Father" but I was puzzled all the way home.

"Latin," I muttered to Jennie. "That prayer is in Latin, so now I'll never find out."

# Walking the Slang Wall

I WAS BORN in my grandfather's house in Thomas Court in the Liberty of St Thomas. The Liberty of St Thomas was the old name, but the area was more commonly called the Earl of Meath's Liberty. Not that the people who lived in and around the Liberty much cared. History was something that belonged in history books, and even then the history of the Liberties of Dublin was never mentioned in Carty's *History of Ireland,* nor by Standish O'Grady. Instead we learned about the Milesians, who said as they approached our shores:

Oh where is the land we have seen in dreams,
Our destined home or grave;
Thus sang they as by the morning's beam
They swept the Atlantic wave.

We heard about the squat, square Fir Bolgs and the magic of the Tuatha de Danaan, all of whom were banished to the mists of the Dublin mountains, and went on to read about the Fianna and the Red Branch knights. History was my favourite subject and I lapped it up, especially the adventure stories. When Art O'Neill made his escape from Dublin Castle, I ran every step of the way with him as he headed for O'Toole and O'Byrne country in the Wicklow hills. Dates were not my strong point and I always mixed up the Young

Irelanders, the United Irishmen and the various rebellions. I preferred the romance of Hugh O'Neill and Red Hugh O'Donnell with their saffron kilts and cloaks, and decided that early history was definitely better than the later stuff.

But our own little streets had their own stories to tell – the streets where we walked and ran. These were the Liberties of Dublin where in times past the great city monasteries had reigned supreme – St Thomas's, St Mary's and the rest. Ours was the Liberty of St Thomas where Henry II of England had raised a great abbey when ordered to do penance for his part in the murder of "that troublesome priest", Thomas à Becket, Archbishop of Canterbury. Here on the outskirts of the city walls the Canons of St Augustine built their church and monastery, their land extending to one hundred acres along the River Poddle. The monks were industrious and set up brewing, tanning, weaving, bacon-curing and leather-making. They governed the people who worked the monastery's land; they made their own laws, exacted taxes, and were responsible only to the king himself.

Four hundred years later Henry VIII, in dispute with the Catholic Church over his many wives, suppressed all monasteries in England and Ireland, and the Abbey of St Thomas and the Liberty were granted to William Brabazon, Under-Treasurer for Ireland. When his grandson was created Earl of Meath, the area became known as the Earl of Meath's Liberty. The family's association with the Liberty is recorded in names like Meath Street, Earl Street, Brabazon Street, Ardee Street and Thirlestane Terrace.

The monks of St Thomas's Abbey, who had been spiritual fathers and temporal landlords to their tenants, were gone. Life went on, as it must. The original brewhouse of the monks at the head of the Coombe – the valley of the Poddle river – had been joined by other small breweries, and the heavy, heady smell of malting hops warmed the coldest winter air. But cattle, horses and livestock crowded beside the small houses and the stench from numerous piggeries, tanneries, abattoirs and animal shelters hung like a heavy mantle above the over-crowded streets. The smell of bread from bakeries which shot steam into the alleys and lanes mingled with the aromas of tobacco, snuff and beer, for alehouses abounded. Little communities huddled together around the Liberty's industries. Houses were shelters with little comfort: clay floors muddied by human traffic and beds of rushes and straw. Rats and mice were constant visitors; rushlights were smelly and candles expensive, so nights dragged on in long hours of darkness.

Then in the late 1600s the Huguenots came and the relative calm of everyday existence was disturbed. They arrived from France, driven out by religious persecution, armed only with their silk-weaving hand-looms. At first the strangers were resented; they were Calvinist, and the majority of the people of the Liberty were Catholic. An uneasy truce was called as the Irish poked at the new silk-weaving looms, which were an innovation compared to their own, and soon they were cheerfully giving their daughters in marriage, in return, no doubt, for another lesson on the silk-loom.

The weaving industry grew and the area prospered. New industries came: tallow-chandlery, glass-making and coach-building. The Huguenots built their strange new houses and the Irish their own terraces side by side. The language became a colourful mixture of the native Gaelic, the settler's English, and the French of the Huguenot.

Street markets and fairs brought life and gaiety, and when the day's work was done people enjoyed their leisure until the watchman's bell proclaimed the end of the day. Aldermen in scarlet, violet and orange robes were splashes of colour in the dirty streets, and the red-coated soldiers, some of them billeted in the Liberty, were daubs of paint against the dull woollen clothes of the poorer people. Chariots, carriages, sedan-chairs and noddies rumbled over uneven roads, and watchmen walked their beats, bellowing the time and news of the day. Church bells rang to call people to prayer and work, to rest and to curfew, and solemnly intoned news of crisis or disaster.

When silk became scarce, the Huguenots married pure wool with their own silk and produced the famous Irish poplin. They dressed the fashionable ladies of Dublin, and Dublin was rapidly gaining a reputation as an exciting city now, for the quality were having one long, glorious ball. But, for the weavers, the good times were short-lived. The industries could not support the thousands who thronged the Liberty streets.

The area went into decline. Tall elegant houses and small cottages overflowed with up to six families sharing one room, the rent determined by the floor space they occupied. The pleasant smells of homely living were replaced by the odours of uncovered and unemptied cess-pits, inadequate sewers and filthy rivers. The stench of sour smelling lime-kilns, rotting herrings, and stale meat from the slaughter-houses began to lie heavy on the air. Living conditions deteriorated. Typhus fever struck in the eighteenth century and cholera in 1834. The Liberty bulged at the seams after the famine of 1845, when refugees from the outlying counties streamed into the city seeking sustenance and relief. Financial crises in Britain affected Ireland and industries closed down. The butterflies of society dipped their wings and fled. Those who cared stayed and helped, and various charitable institutions were set up, but the famous, all-embracing weaving industry and its ancillary industries were lost.

The brewing industry, however, weathered the storm, as might perhaps be expected; gathering together in small taverns was the consolation of the poor. The brewers prospered and none more so than Arthur Guinness, who had started business quietly and modestly with one mash tun, one seventy-barrel copper, and one acre of land. By the time my grandfather arrived in the Liberty of St Thomas, all that had changed. The Guinness brewery had grown into an empire.

WANT AND HUNGER still stalked the streets when my grandfather, my mother's father, came to Dublin in the mid-1870s from a small farm in Kyle in the soft boggy hills of West Wicklow. He and his older brother had left the land to find work in the city, and approached the brewery of Arthur Guinness, Son and Company, the biggest employers in Dublin. Grandfather would have had some sort of reference from Lord Fitzwilliam of Coollattin estate.

"Big powerful landlords," my father would say. "They have the whole country between them. Between the Fitzwilliams at Coollattin, the Oranmore and Brownes at Luggala, the Lord Powerscourts, the Meaths at Bray and the La Touches at Greystones, there's little left for the peasants."

My grandfather became a drayman with the brewery, and he lived in one of the trust-houses built by Arthur Guinness for some of his workers. His lot was a good one. He had a steady job with one of the best employers in the country, good money as a drayman, and security, for a job in Guinness's brewery was "money dead or alive". The brewery paid its workforce while they were ill, looked after them in their illnesses and gave them a pension when they retired. Above all, a job in Guinness's gave respectability.

My grandmother was one of seven sisters. She also came from Kyle, but farther down the valley on the road to

Ballinglen. One of the "loveliest set of women to walk up the Kyle Road", my grandfather would say, and she did look a beauty in the photographs we had of her and Grandfather. The face that looked out from the ornate frames was serene and gracious. I also thought she looked slightly disdainful, but I kept this view to myself. Her gown of brocade had leg-of-mutton sleeves and rows of tiny buttons from neck to waist and from elbow to wrist. There was beaded braiding on the pinched-in waist, with the taffeta silk skirt flaring over the hips.

Then Grandmother died, a victim of a bad outbreak of 'flu in 1914, leaving my mother, at fourteen years of age, to keep house for her father. It was an accepted fact of Dublin life that on the death of a mother the eldest or only daughter left school or work to tend the remaining family. Around her my mother had cousins whose parents had also come from the country and neighbours who had migrated from Meath and Wexford to set up homes in and around South Earl Street, Thomas Court and Thomas Court Bawn.

The little community was expanding. Homes strained to accommodate yet more country neighbours while they found their feet in the crowded city. My father, in his turn, arrived in Dublin in search of work. His home had been in Tinahely in County Wicklow, about seven miles from my mother's parents' townland, though my parents had never met one another there. My father loved horses and he, too, found work as a drayman, working first as an assistant and later, after he had married, in charge of his own horse and dray, delivering minerals for Cantrell & Cochrane of St Stephen's Green.

I thought my mother was beautiful. She took great care with her appearance both inside and outside the home. Her hair was dark and thick. It fell straight to her shoulders, and when it needed cutting my father or one of her cousins snipped it for her. She wound it into a knot and wore it flat at the back of her head or in a top-knot which she held in place with brown clips and fine hairpins, patted into place over her ears, but never drawn back in a severe sweep. Her eyes were dark brown and big in her face. She was slim and looked taller than she was because of her slimness and because she held her head straight. A spotlessly clean bib was an essential part of her everyday dress and she had a selection for working around the house. She wore long straight skirts, sometimes slit at the end, or with a big pleat to one side. She favoured brown or grey pinstripe flannel or tweed skirts with high-collared silk, cotton or satin blouses. She always wore a hat outdoors and her coat was slim-fitting and flared from the waist. In the studio pictures which stood on the parlour mantelpiece, she wore a low-cut "glad-neck" blouse with a narrow neckband of velvet ribbon on which a cameo brooch was centred. In spring and summer she wore a bodice-hugging dark costume and in winter she added a fox-fur slung over one shoulder.

When my parents married it made sense for them to live in my grandfather's house, but when I was born, the fourth in the family, although my sister had died, they felt it was time to buy a home of their own – the existing home in Thomas Court was too small.

"Your grandfather, God be good to him, never liked the move. His heart was in Thomas Court," my godmother Lily told me. My parents' move took him four miles from his beloved streets, to Inchicore, a suburb on the west of the city.

"It was an unlucky move," my mother always said. It should have been for the best – they were buying their own home – but nobody seemed to be too happy. Then without warning my father became unemployed due to economic recession. Unemployment was biting into every home, with sometimes fathers and sons in the same household losing their jobs.

We moved back to the Liberty again, not back to the old streets, but near enough for all the adults to be close to the old community. The move gave my grandfather a new lease of life.

Our house was one of about 200 new dwellings built by the Corporation in the early 1930s on a field between the Grand Canal and the lovely village of Dolphin's Barn, known as the home of Dolfyn the Dane. In Irish it was known as *Carnan Cloc*. In ancient Dublin records it is given as the Rock or Hill of the Clann Dunphy. Dunphy was King of Leinster, whose boundaries stretched to *Carnan Cloc*.

The houses were separated from the fields above us by what was known as the Back of the Pipes and the Slang Wall. The Back of the Pipes was a walk-way which started at Dolphin's Barn and ran at the back of the houses on Emerald Square and along one side of Cork Street, then past an open space until it reached Malin Avenue. On the other side it was bordered by the Slang Wall, and beyond that wall was the little River Slang, one of the many arms of the Poddle river, where the boys fished for pinkeens with nets and jam-jars.

The Poddle flowed beneath a little hump-backed bridge on Dolphin's Barn Street, through Patterson's yard, and was then piped underground, leaving us an open space on which to play. The river broke ground again and flowed past the back of Jennie's house. In later years it was piped there, too, as part of the city's watercourse.

"It's been known as the Back of the Pipes for generations," Mr Boylan, whose family had owned land around the area, told my father. "The pipes for the watercourse always came down here." Mr Boylan claimed that the Poddle was the busiest river in the city, it had so many streams and arms and people claiming it for their own in so many different places.

But it was the Slang Wall and not the river which was a

nightmare for our parents. When the playground was occupied by boys kicking ball, we liked to play on the grass of the Poddle's open space.

"Queeney case, who has the ball?" We were ringed around Ann who stood with her back to us, ready to throw the ball over her head for one of us to catch. But with a wild swoop she sent the ball sailing over the Slang Wall behind where we stood. Our hands, cupped to receive the ball, dropped to our sides.

"It's my ball – I want it back!" John, who lived at the end of the road, didn't usually play in our games, but he had been enticed to join because he was the only one with a ball.

"I'll get it for you."

"But it's gone over the Slang Wall," Jennie pointed out. "You'll never find it."

"I'll try," I called as I scrambled up, my knees gripping the rough stones and my fingers scrabbling for a hold. The wall was ten feet high, or so we told one another. Anyway, it was as high as Mr Railway Man, who was the tallest man on our road, and he could only see over the top of the wall if he stood on tippy-toes. When I reached the top I looked into the fields beyond and below me the little River Slang: if I fell in there I would be in real trouble. Mary and Ann climbed up beside me. I gathered myself up, crouched forward and jumped. I landed clear of the water and found the ball stuck under a clump of dandelions. I threw the ball back, but the game of Queenie was abandoned – the next challenge was on. Who would go furthest along the wall until we were caught or somebody fell off? When they built the Slang Wall they had not intended to make it easy for us, and blocks stood up at regular intervals, forcing us to step up and over them, but once we found our feet we strutted proudly along the top. There was no pushing or shoving: that was the rule of the game. The next challenge was to pass each other, and as we passed we held on to one another, placing each foot carefully around the other, balancing delicately until there was a shout – "There's somebody coming" – and we scrambled down, straightening our cotton dresses and smoothing down our hair, and hoping we looked the way little girls were supposed to and not like rowdy tomboys.

# The Keys Around My Neck

M Y MOTHER LIKED to talk about her schooldays. Often she would refer to the fact that she had to leave school before her time.

"They wanted me to become a monitress." She sighed as she flicked the crotchet hook through the lace collar she was shaping.

"What was a monitress?"

"We didn't call them teachers like you do," she answered. "Our teachers were mistresses and the monitors and monitresses were like student teachers."

"Sounds posh. Was it posh?" My mother looked at me, no doubt wondering what impression her words were having on my imagination.

"Well," she said, "no school was posh in those days, but they gave good schooling," she went on proudly. "We had to wear a sort of uniform – little white pinnies over our own clothes."

My mother attended School Street school, the first Model School of the Kildare Place Society. It had originally been a Sunday school, set up in the late eighteenth century by the rector of the parish with assistance from the Earl of Meath. He gathered the girls of the area into a parochial hall, while the boys were given the use of the courthouse in Thomas Court Bawn. The school was held on Sundays initially, and the children were taught the three R's; the girls were also taught how to sew, with materials supplied to them, and they were allowed to take home the clothes they made. Scripture was read to them, but without comment. In the early 1900s School Street opened as a full-time day school due to the intervention of Mr Ephraim Bewley of the Society of Friends, and became the first "free" school in the area.

"It wasn't a Catholic school, you know," my mother said. She always referred to it as a secular school.

"Then why were you sent there?"

"Because I only had to go round the corner. And then all the children from there went – these were the shopkeepers' and the publicans' children. It wasn't too easy to get into the school – you had to have a reference from somebody like a publican or a householder." She paused while she measured the crotchet collar.

"I suppose you're wondering how we were taught our religion. Well, on a Sunday morning we had to go to Meath Street chapel after the last Mass to learn our catechism, or we'd have been in trouble with the priests. We got merits when we got our answers right. And so many merits meant that you could claim a prize, either a holy picture or a prayer-book."

With us it was going to be different. My mother was intelligent, gifted in many ways and possessed of a great natural dignity, but she had been denied the freedom of an independent life. Now she had to make a choice as to where we would go to school.

"I want to send the children to the nuns," she told my father.

"Well, ye have a chance now," he said; "there's a right clatter of them around us for you to choose."

The decision, as in all these things, would be my mother's. She did the planning and could see straight ahead to the ultimate result. Father was her sounding-post. I never heard him oppose any decision she made in our regard, but he was not behind the door in pointing out the pitfalls.

"Remember," he said, "the Loreto school on the Crumlin Road and the Holy Faiths below on the Coombe are right foreigners. You don't want the childer soaked on a wet mornin' before they hit the top of the Pipes or find their way to the Coombe." She listened carefully to what he had to say.

"It looks like Cork Street convent then," she said.

"The best of luck to you so," he said. "I hear it's not easy get a place there; that school has a great name. You could," he said, warming to the idea, "you could look for a letter from the priest. We live in the parish."

That was not the way my mother intended to go about it. She drummed on the kitchen table.

"What's the chance of gettin' to see the school before I make up my mind?"

"Not a hope in hell," my father said, but he recognised the determined look in my mother's eye and was not surprised when she put on her good brown costume, settled her straw hat firmly on her head and said she was about to interview the principal of the school.

"A tyrant, Missus, she is. She'll give ye short shrift." My mother, who never listened to such remarks but formed her own impression of people, was not put off by Sister Magdalen's reputation. The Mercy Sisters' convent school stood in Weaver's Square, its big front gate and drive facing on to Cork Street. We rarely saw this gate open; entrance was gained through a small door in Weaver's Square.

Mothers were not encouraged to come past the school gate. Crying children were collected by the "big" girls and cajoled or bullied into their classrooms. Then the school gate was locked and guard was kept on it by the big girls who questioned all late-comers through a grille at the top of the door.

Sister Magdalen turned sharply when my mother's knock sounded on her office door. She pushed back her black veil and bristled forward. "Mothers," she said, "are not allowed past the schoolyard. It's ten o'clock," and she glanced at the wall clock at the side of the office door. "How did you get in here?"

"I came through the convent gate and across the schoolyard," my mother told her serenely, perfectly aware of the trespass she had committed. Sister Magdalen looked sharply at her. Such temerity and initiative on the part of a mother was unexpected. They took one another's measure, the short dynamic custodian of the school and the tall woman whose great concern was her children's education. Each liked what she saw, and a common ground was established between them which was to last until the end of our schooldays.

When my mother returned home she could hardly conceal her sense of triumph.

"I got a tour of the school," she told my father. He looked at her over the rim of his reading glasses. "I did," she said; "she showed me everywhere."

Sister Magdalen had treated her like a visiting inspector, throwing open classroom doors and halting lessons in midsentence. My mother relived the story of that day many times. It had boosted her confidence and her belief that she must always look for the best for her children.

"That Sister Magdalen has a heart of gold when you take her the right way. She's soft underneath and lives for the good of you children and the school. I don't," she warned each of us sternly, "ever want to hear a bad word said against her."

It seemed to us that the Sister Magdalen we knew and the

one my mother liked and respected could not be one and the same. The Sister Magdalen we knew ruled with a rod of iron from her little crowded office just inside the main door at the foot of the big stone stairs. Every message, every absentee's excuse, all copy books and readers purchased passed through her hands, and woe betide anyone who arrived a minute past nine-thirty. The door was locked and the late-comer stood outside her door until she was ready to deal with them. When she moved from classroom to classroom during the school day, we knew she was coming by the sound of the jangling keys eternally suspended from the leather strap at her waist. Her authority was absolute. Even her own teachers, I always felt, were in awe of her.

Four of us left for school each morning when we started in Weaver's Square, two sisters older and one younger than me. Later on we were joined by Nance and Tess. We met with Jennie and her sisters, Anne and Maddy with their brothers and sisters, and we streamed out into Vauxhall Avenue, past the high factory wall on one side. There was no other way to school except on shank's mare, and as some of the shank's mares in our group were rather shorter than others, it was a slow journey. At the end of the avenue we came to Cork Street, a long narrow cobbled street which joined Dolphin's Barn Street at Thornton's dairy. There was a little hump in the road at that point which had once been a bridge, and it was said the tanners in the twelfth century had washed their skins in the tributary of the River Poddle which flowed beneath it. If we climbed the wall of Patterson's pig-yard across from the dairy, we could see a portion of the little river. We climbed the wall anyway to watch the pigs, hold our noses and complain loudly of the smell.

Timmons's coal-yard was a few houses down from the piggery. A dusty black film hung over everything in and around the yard's tiny shop, which had a low door from which Mr Timmons would emerge covered in coal dust. He was a huge man and filled the whole doorway. He seemed to be on the go in all weathers, arms bared in summer and with a coal-sack tied over his shoulders in winter. His black-rimmed eyes looked out good-humouredly from a handsome face as he backed his dray across the cobbles. His children's black curly heads bobbed in and out of the shop as they helped to measure and shovel the buckets of coal. Not everybody could afford to buy coal by the bag, so Mr Timmons also sold it by the bucket, and a steady trail of coal dust led out of his yard as his customers struggled homewards with their loads.

We turned left into Cork Street and were immediately faced with a choice of routes. One way brought us along the upper part of Cork Street, which had fine two-storey houses on one side, but beyond these houses lay the skin-yard.

"I don't care if it takes you all day to go to school the other way, you don't go near the skin-yard." Our mother's instructions were clear, but curiosity often tempted us to ignore them. I was never quite sure what they did in the skin-yard. Carts rolled up to the gates with smelly fleeces and the dark black skins of cattle all lashed together in a solid mass. Maggots crawled in the blood outside the yard. Terror-stricken by the sickening maggots, I never tried to look behind the yard's big wooden gates.

On the corner opposite the skin-yard stood Devlin's sweet factory. Strangely, I hated the smell from the factory – it was sickly sweet and somehow hung in the air and followed you as you went through the little cottages out to Donore Avenue. This was a lonely way to school because at the top of Brown Street we came to the gate of the Fever Hospital's death house. The gate was always closed.

"They don't let e'er a soul see through it," Jennie said as we hurried past; "it's bad luck if ye do." Brown Street was a grey old street with nothing interesting on it, and it always seemed to be empty of people. The screeching of the pigs at the back of Donnelly's factory in Brickfield Lane added to the eeriness of the place, with the high wall of the hospital a constant reminder of the fever which was still held in dread. Eventually we came to the most elegant building in the street, the firm of Elliott's, the poplin makers, which had granite steps to its door.

"Elliott's is a very famous place," Sister Ignatius told us. "They weave poplin in there – poplin ties and scarves and lovely vestments. You know, children, this was a great weaving area." But ties and scarves and weavers were far from our thoughts as we trudged back and forth with our schoolbags on our backs.

Our other way to school, which took us down Cork Street, was much more interesting, because this was on the main route to the city centre. Buses passed us by at intervals but we gave them hardly a thought, as our young legs were made for walking. We did worry more about the horses, because on frosty November days or snowy January mornings they brought great excitement to our school-going. The cobbles on the street were treacherous, especially when we had black frost, and the horses slipped going down Cork Street and had to struggle coming up. Every dray carried pieces of sacking and twine to wrap around the horses' hooves, and we never had any hesitation in abandoning schoolbags and giving the cart a push whether we were needed or not. We willingly helped carry kettles of water from shops to thaw out the frozen stones, and cheerfully scattered handfuls of salt and soot, ending up with our woollen gloves sodden and streaked with grime.

"I dare you," became a favourite game as we hunched our

school satchels higher on our shoulders and pulled up our woollen stockings for the long walk. Children of the family who owned a public house on Cork Street passed us on their way to the Young Ladies' College on the Crumlin Road, where they wore lovely green uniforms of pleated gym-frocks, blazers and caps emblazoned in gold. Some devil prompted me as we went by the open door of the pub. Usually a few men with mufflers criss-crossed about their collarless shirts would be hanging around the closed door, or a woman hovering in the near-distance, a jug clutched under her shawl, but this morning it stood wide open and we stopped to look in. Women and children were not allowed into a public bar except for a little place called a snug, where women could be served drink while in the company of a man or have a jug filled to take home.

"I dare you," said Jennie. I put my foot on the first step and hesitated. "I dare you" came again and then a push. Daring and pushing were twin sisters. If you accepted a dare, you were helped to its execution by willing hands. My foot caught on the inner step and I sprawled across the floor, my nose and mouth caked in brown sawdust which smelled of sour porter. My head landed inches from the trailing shawl of an old woman whose jug the publican had been surreptitiously filling.

"The Lord between us and all harm, mind me man's jug a' porter," she squealed.

"Sorry, Ma'am," I managed to gasp. I hadn't a chance. A hand gripped my schoolbag and hauled me to my feet, while my pencil-case spilled its wooden pen handle and precious nibs and pencils across the floor.

"Where do you go to school?" The dreaded question. Never "who are you?" or "where do you live?" School was the highest authority.

"Weaver's Square," I croaked, as I adjusted the bow on the back of my head which my mother had carefully placed there not half-an-hour before. I scrubbed the sawdust from my face and knees and bent to pick up my nibs and pen.

"I'm sorry, Mister," I croaked again, "it was only a dare. Please don't tell on me."

"Get out of my shop," he roared. "I'll be on to the nuns; see if I don't."

There wasn't one friend in sight when I stumbled from the shop, the beginnings of a hole in my long stockings. But I knew where they were, hiding in doorways just beyond the public house. I didn't know who had pushed me and I didn't care, I just sailed past, my head held high and my honour intact. I made no reply to their anxious enquiries but for days afterwards every time we rose to greet Sister Magdalen with "*Dia dhuit, a Shiúr,*" I froze where I stood, waiting to be summoned to her office.

A week later I was on my way home and from a distance away I saw the publican standing at his door. There was no way by except to pass him, either on his side of the road or mine. Maybe, I prayed, he has forgotten. Let him be blind, I prayed, and not see me. I kept my head down.

"You," he said as I drew level, "is this yours?" I looked up in surprise. "Here," he said, and in his hand he had my precious nib-box.

"Don't ever try anything like that again," he warned me, and he turned on his heel.

I didn't dare open the nib-box until I was safely home. Inside he had placed a lovely new shiny N-nib.

Our school was big, cold and draughty. In winter the iron radiators groaned all day and never got really hot. We hawed with hot breaths and knuckled up the sleeves of our jumpers to clear startlingly beautiful patterns of ice from the window panes. Bad weather rarely kept us away from school. On the coldest days we were allowed keep our coats, caps and gloves on in class, while the nuns wrapped black shawls around their shoulders and drew finger-less gloves over their hands while they worked.

I liked school. In Babies and High Babies we sat snugly together and made funny shapes from *márla*, and got tapped on the knuckles if we mashed the colours together in a rainbow mess, which I was particularly fond of doing. We sorted *cipíní* into various colours and stuck wallpaper on to matchboxes with gooey paste from a big jar, and built up sets of drawers and poked gold drawing pins into them for handles. We snuggled down quietly when the teacher got tired of all our shifting round in our desks and told us to go to sleep, and at break we lined up for the dash to the lavatories across the open play-yard of the school. Order and discipline reigned as we rhymed aloud and in unison, chanting the names of the rivers and towns of Ireland and Europe, the amount of shillings, pence, ha'pence and farthings in a pound, pints and quarts in a gallon, and how many roods and perches made an acre. We sang out our tables in Irish, *a haon is a haon sin a dó*, but our first real singing lesson came when we were herded into the next classroom and pushed into seats between older sisters as Miss Alford marched across the boards, struck her tuning fork against the iron radiator, held it aloft and hummed:

"Lah-ti-doh-soh-me-doh. Me, me, me. Now, girls, deep breaths and all together," and her arms swung out and up and swooped on the singing chart which hung over the blackboard. Up and down the scales we went, while Miss Alford used her hands to signal tones and semi-tones. Then she listened to sections of the class in turn, jabbing her tuning fork accusingly at anyone who might be croaking like a frog.

"I DON'T WANT to go," I told my mother when I came home from school with the bit of paper which said I was now passing into Miss Healy's class and listed the books I would need.

My mother looked at me. She had heard tales of Miss Healy from Madge and Babs, who had already passed through her hands.

"She's the best teacher in the school," my mother said, pleased that her number three had made the grade.

"She's also the best cane-hitter in the school," I whimpered. All teachers had a cane but they rarely used it; it was a symbol of authority and the sound of its swishing was enough to quell the most rebellious heart. Miss Healy was the exception.

"You won't get the cane unless you need it, and that's entirely up to you," my mother said, busy with one hundred and one other tasks.

"Maybe you'll get to carry her cases," Jennie consoled me on our way to school that morning.

I was nervous but prepared to take what came my way, and kept reminding myself that this teacher turned out the best girls in the school. Miss Healy ruled with a rod of iron, and catechism time was when she came into her own. She perched herself on a desk in the front row with her knees uncomfortably close to the girls in the desk below her, and having pushed two children into one seat to make room for her. From this vantage point she could touch everybody in the class with her cane or with the long blackboard pointer. She had another weapon also: a coloured pencil.

"You see this marker, girls?" She held it up. "There is not another like it in the whole school. Do you understand that, girls?" To our chorus of "Yes, Miss," she went on, "These markers are especially made for me and I get them in a special box." She displayed a little cardboard box full of similar pink pencils.

"When you have answered your catechism question correctly I will mark your book with a tick. Nobody else in the school can do that for you, because this pencil is a special colour, so don't anybody ever dare to mark their catechism questions or answers themselves."

Of course there were those who did, the hardened sinners at the back of the class who had more nerve than the rest of us. They were caught each time, but they felt it was worth it just to see Miss Healy's explosion of spluttering rage at the audacity of those who had sought to question the authority of her magenta-pink marker.

Yet Miss Healy had a wide and generous heart and the eccentricity of a creative mind. For St Patrick's Day she made the most splendid badges for each of the fifty or so children in her class. They were large paper confections made from brilliantly coloured silver papers with intricate cut-out designs, layer on layer, and no two were the same. She never asked a penny for them and we were proud to wear them on our national feast day.

Her method of teaching was thorough. All our exercise copies were carried to her home in two or three cases, methodically marked with the secret pencil, and brought back again in the morning. The best girls in the class had the honour of carrying the cases.

"You, girl," she pointed to me one day when I had been bright at answering questions, "you can carry my cases in the morning. You know where I live; be at the house at a quarter to nine."

My mother wasn't a bit pleased. "Those cases will drag the guts out of ye," she said. But there wasn't much she could do. If she complained she felt it might go against me in school, and she knew I was rather proud that I had been selected. There were two of us to do the carrying and one of us would be the custodian, not only of the cases, but also of Miss Healy's bundle of keys. The girl who took charge of the keys wore them on a cord around her neck, so everybody in the play-yard knew how important she was.

I set out next morning for the mile-long walk to Miss Healy's home. The cases were ready at the hall-door, and I was given the keys. Mary and I set off. Down the street we went and around the corner, half carrying, half dragging the heavy cases. It was a long walk to the school and it would take us every minute of the half-hour she had allowed for us to reach it. We shifted the weight from one hand to another, struggling with our schoolbags. Coming into Cow Parlour and nearly in sight of the school I decided I'd had enough. I plonked my case down and sat on it to take a rest.

"You can't do that," Mary said in alarm.

"Why can't I?" My hand was raw from the leather handle.

"Because she'll be around the corner in a minute and she'll catch you."

"I don't care," I said truculently. "Why doesn't she carry her old cases herself?"

"I might have known I couldn't trust you to do a simple task." She marched up, the bright intelligent eyes under the auburn permed hair, looking disdainfully at my forlorn figure.

"Pick up that case and follow me," she commanded. I did, but I dragged it and bumped it to the school gate where she was waiting. She said nothing as she rescued her precious case, but I was stripped of the jangling keys, my day of glory disappearing in one stroke.

Miss Healy was one of the teachers who most shaped my school life, but it was in Fourth Class with Sister de Paul that my love of performing was developed. She was a big, stout, red-faced nun, whose starched white wimple seemed to give her constant aggravation. She was light on her feet and skipped swiftly between the rows of desks, encouraging us as we recited poetry, which was her big passion. Sometimes we were sent to give displays of our dramatic recitals to other classrooms and to the Dublin *Feis* held in Marlboro' Street in the city centre.

In the confines of the classroom she ignored all the laws of order and discipline and helped us push the desks back against the wall so that she could stage Padraig Pearse's *Íosagán* and *Na Bóithre*. These dramas were acted out with extravagant displays of swinging arms and clutching breasts, wringing hands and keening voices; in her excitement Sister de Paul's black veil would go askew, her wimple twist sideways, and a strand of black hair would escape.

"Stop tittering, girls," she said as she pushed the offending hair back.

"I thought she was bald." Mary was spluttering behind her hand. "Janey mac, I thought they were all bald!"

"I thought they got it all shaved off when they became nuns." Joan stood with her mouth open as she watched Sister de Paul adjust the white cap.

"Enough's enough now; back with the desks, girls, and mind you don't spill over the inkwells."

It was in Sister de Paul's class, too, that we got the best value from the student teachers, whose arrival was a welcome break in the boredom of the long school year. They were different faces and personalities from the black-robed nuns and the impersonal teachers, and we loved every single one of them for a fortnight. There was a mystery about them that we liked. Nobody explained who they were or why they came to the school, and perhaps there was good reason for that. To tell us that they were in fact trainee teachers learning their trade might be tempting fate in a crowded high-spirited class. When some bright spark found out in Fourth Class that some of the students were only about six years older than ourselves, our respect for them began to diminish a little. The sense of mystery remained, however, because they came from a far-away place called Carysfort College, and, if we were to believe some of the know-alls in the class, from the richest families in the country.

"Their families are rollin' in it," a sage in the back row declared vigorously.

"Who says so?"

"My dad swears to it."

"Your dad'd swear a hole through an iron pot."

"But she's right," another joined in. "They pay huge fees to be teachers."

"You're havin' us on. Who'd pay money to teach us?"

Sister Magdalen's announcement that the students were coming was greeted with a ripple of excited chatter.

"Silence, girls. In a week's time the students will be here. I want everybody on their best behaviour. Do I make myself clear?" Sister Magdalen always made herself clear but liked to hear us say so. "I want them to be able to say when they leave that this was the best school they ever taught in."

"I hope they get value for their money," came a comment from the back of the class.

The next week was spent making ours the shiniest school in the country, never mind the city. Every child brought a clean rag or duster and a lump of polish purloined from the tin at home, or the tin itself if a mother was feeling generous. We were sent to our tasks like an army of little cleaners: one girl to take the china grey inkwells to the big sink near the lavatories to wash them in icy cold water; another sent round to refill them with a big earthenware jug of ink.

"Dust the legs of your desks, girls, and no comics under the desks."

"I've my good Sunday dress on," Maddy complained. "If I get a speck on it dusting the silly old desks, who's going to help my mother clean it?" But suddenly she changed her tune. "Yes, Sister, certainly, Sister, I won't forget to dust the window-sills," and Maddy polished harder than ever under the eye of Sister de Paul.

Our classroom in the Far East, nicknamed after the missions towards which we put our pennies in the nodding black-babies boxes, was the vantage point from which we could watch the students parade through the convent grounds at ten o'clock each morning.

Two by two the students came, dressed in ankle-length black serge dresses and clutching their boxes and papers to their chests. They wore taffeta ribbons, with different colours to denote the student's year and a large medal of Our Lady suspended from the bottom. The Reverend Mother of the convent, who was seen only on special occasions, led them in a stately procession across the yard and into the school. Two students were allocated to each class, a senior who took the lesson while the junior sat in the last seat taking notes.

An air of high tension gripped the school: once the students had arrived, examiners and inspectors would soon follow. The students were being assessed as part of their training, but this also was a test for the school, and in any case the nuns were firmly on the students' side. Our classroom became the centre of strategy for the following days, and Sister de Paul took on the responsibility of alerting the other classes as to when, how and where the examining professors would strike. We were her look-outs, peeping over window-sills, loitering casually beside doors, and popping inquisitive eyes over partition windows. When we spotted an examiner we flew upstairs and ran like things demented along corridors to sound the alarm. We hid behind pillars and presses and once, having panicked at the sound of approaching voices, I managed to get shut in amongst the coats in the cloakroom when Sister Magdalen, seeing an open door, closed it firmly against me.

Everybody was in on the act of getting the students through their test and school fell flat for a long time after they left us. It was with great sadness that we waved to them as their bus lurched out of the convent gate and turned down to the Coombe.

# Walking Taller

SCHOOL AND HOME joined together to prepare us for the sacraments of Holy Communion and Confirmation. The nuns took on the responsibility of turning us out as good Catholic children, strong in our faith and prepared to die for it if necessary. I listened to their tales of martyrs and saints, secretly glad those days were over because I was pretty sure that I would not be up to scratch, and I did not want anybody to find out that I was a coward at heart.

As they helped me prepare for the sacrament of penance and Holy Communion, my older sisters were intensely interested in my Confession.

"I didn't steal the sugar." I was indignant, my voice rising in a wail of protest.

"We know you didn't," Madge and Babs soothed. "It doesn't matter, just say it anyway. It just means that if you did and you have forgotten, then your sin will be forgiven."

"Let's start again." Babs sat sideways on one of the kitchen chairs, while I knelt by the bars at the back. "Say it again," she instructed.

"Bless me, Father, for I have sinned, this is my First Confession."

"Yes, my child," she intoned in the deepest voice she could muster. I looked at her in disdain.

"You don't sound like the priest."

"I'll give ye a puck if ye don't get on with it," the "priest" retorted sharply.

"I stole the sugar three times. I told a lot of lies. I pulled my sister's hair and I gave back-answers... what are back-answers?"

"It means you were cheeky."

"But I wasn't cheeky."

"You were, two minutes ago."

"It doesn't matter," Madge tried to calm things down. "You tell the priest all these things – then it means you haven't forgotten anything and he will give you absolution."

I, who when I was sick had been half a minute in the next world, was always very careful to keep a tab on the number of lies I told, but my sisters were eager to tag on all kinds of sins I was sure I had never committed. As they had been through it already, I granted that they knew what they were talking about, and they considered it their duty as big sisters to see that I was well-rehearsed in everything I had to say and do.

The excitement of First Communion day was overshadowed for weeks by the preparation for First Confession. I knew the confessionals: they were the mysterious little rooms at the side of the church where the priest hid behind a dark curtain while people queued outside, waiting their turns to confess their sins. I had waited in the chapel on Saturday mornings while my sisters made their confessions, smug in the knowledge that I didn't yet have to brave the terrors of the darkness and the unknown.

First Confessions were made in the convent chapel adjoining the school. Hat, coat and gloves were set out for me the night before by my mother, as no girl was allowed enter the chapel with an uncovered head. We had been joined by the boys from Brown Street, so there were about seventy of us for Confession in all.

All eyes were focused on the confessional. I was glad to see it was less frightening than the ones in our church; the priest sat with the curtain partly drawn back so that he could be seen by the apprehensive six- and seven-year-olds taking their first step towards responsible childhood.

Jennie and I made our First Confessions together. I was cold that May day and shivered as we tip-tapped across the polished wooden floor, genuflecting to the bright red sanctuary lamp which hung like a welcoming eye in front of the altar. "Don't make noise, children," was hissed at us in giant whispers as we shuffled in relays into our seats. We were drawn well back from the confessional and brought up one by one when our turn came.

"You," I nudged Joan in the seat beside me, "don't you listen to my sins." Joan was so petrified she didn't hear me. I was terrified that I would speak in too loud a voice and everybody would know how bad I really was. It didn't matter with the priest because, when your confession was over, he forgot everything you told him.

"That's a special grace he gets," we were told by Sister Genevieve. That was all very well with the priest. God looked after that part for you, but what about the teacher and the nun? They did not get the same grace, and what if they heard all the bad things you had done and remembered them the next time you tried to tell a white lie?

When my turn came I stood on the little step in the box and in a high squeaky voice recited my sins as duly instructed by my sisters. I waited. Not a sound came from the priest. I stared into the blackness behind the grille. He was still there, so I had not been shouting at an empty space. I poked my head closer.

"Father!" I whispered loudly.

A deep sigh escaped from the priest. The whiteness of his

face turned towards me and to my relief he raised his hand and murmured the Latin prayers. I stumbled out of the box.

"Go up to the altar rails and say your penance," Sister Genevieve hissed into my ear. I glanced anxiously at her as her hand gripped my arm. She smiled reassuringly.

"You do remember what the priest gave you for your penance?"

Penance? Oh, God. What had the priest said when he turned to me that time? My mind skidded backwards. In my relief at the confession being over and the knowledge that I had not given the priest a heart attack with my spiel of sins, I had nearly forgotten. Now it came to me.

"That's a good girl," he had said. "Now I'll bless your rosary for you if you'll hold it up. And for your penance you can say…" I looked at Sister Genevieve and nodded, and I thought how clever that priest was, even if his mind had been elsewhere. He hadn't been at all cross either. "For your penance, you can say the first prayer that comes into your head."

While the nuns took care of the spiritual side of things, my mother was the one who had to look after my material needs. It was important that everything be right for the big day. Preparations started in February. There was a white dress to be selected, a new coat big enough to last a couple of winters, white socks, white shoes and all new underwear, and it would be shop underwear this time. A wreath and veil would only be worn on the day itself, so the purchase of a straw hat for Sunday Mass would complete the outfit.

"Can I have black patent shoes?" I asked as we started out one Saturday morning for Thomas Street.

"No, you cannot. Everything except the coat must be white for Holy Communion."

"Marie is getting black patent shoes. Her mother says they're a lot easier to keep clean."

"She's entitled to her opinion," my mother smiled at me, "but you're my child and you're having white buckskin shoes. You can whiten them every Saturday night for Sunday." She paused. "Jennie's getting white buckskin, too. I was talking to her mother yesterday."

That softened my disappointment a little, but having lost out on the shoes, I tried again.

"Can I have a long white dress? With a cloak and white fur around the collar? Mam," I tugged at her arm, "did ye hear me?"

"I was just thinkin'," she said, "that there's the dress your sister had for the Guinness concert last year. The one that Babs wore when she said that poem about 'The Rake up Near the Rafters'. It looked very nice on the stage. I would have to put a few tucks in it because you're so skinny, but it would do you nicely for the day. It wasn't a bad little dress."

I stopped in my tracks. She couldn't; she wouldn't do this to me for my First Holy Communion, my first big day ever. I stayed silent for the rest of the journey, just as she had intended.

"Let's try this." She had gone through a rail of dresses at Frawley's and stopped at one. She examined it carefully – the seams for letting out, the length of the hem for letting down. I tried it on, and loved it so much I was afraid to budge.

"How much?" Satisfied with the price, she turned and twisted me round again. "Like it?" she asked. She didn't have to ask a second time. I was like a little princess.

The wreath and veil was my godmother's present to me, and there was only one shop in Dublin where it could be purchased to suit both my godmother and my mother. "Kellett's in George's Street. They have the best wreaths in Dublin an' make no mistake about it."

My mother watched their window, full of hats and veils,

53

toques, half-veils, turbans and straws which changed colours with the season and the half-season. She watched it through the wedding season when Kellet's dazzled with white satin, silks, shantung, crêpe de Chine and broderie anglaise, and the diamante head-dresses winked in the mirrored windows.

"Oceans and oceans of tulle and laces and net." My mother's face lit up at the memory. "The girl told me the Holy Communion things will be in next week."

Shoes and gloves were left till nearer the big day.

"Three months is a long time and at the rate you're springin' up your feet could grow a whole size bigger. And we can't chance gettin' them too big. We don't want you sliggin' your shoes to the chapel if they're not the right size."

If I couldn't have black patent shoes and the long dress had been banished to the realms of the ridiculous, I could at least have a go at the white socks.

"Can I have shop socks?"

"No."

"Why?"

"They're too expensive and don't last jig-time." My mother was not the only one who prided herself on knitting ankle-socks. She knitted them from silk skeins of thread which matched all the colours of the rainbow.

"Please don't get me silk-crêpe." This was a new thread on the market and stronger than the ordinary silk. "The crêpe hurts the soles of my feet."

"It's hard-wearing," she said.

"And you don't have to wear them," I muttered under my breath. So we settled for the white silk and my mother made white elastic garters to hold them up, because hand-knitted silks soon lost their shape and flopped around your ankles. Because everything must be perfect for this Holy Communion Day, there was no careless guessing of widths and lengths. I had to stay close to the house while mother knitted the socks on four steel needles.

"Put your foot carefully through those needles and don't wriggle or the stitches will come off." Cautiously I slipped my toes down the narrow tunnel of the sock's leg and negotiated the turn in the heel, sighing for the luxury of machine-made socks. They were finished with an intricate open-work pattern, carefully washed and laid on layers of blue paper to dry. Drying on a line would drag them out of shape.

The First Holy Communion Mass was at nine o'clock on the last Saturday in May. I had been scrubbed from head to toe in the old aluminium bath in front of the fire the night before. My new underclothes were carefully laid out on the kitchen chair.

"I've got butterflies in my tummy," I wailed as I stood in my nightdress at the kitchen door.

"Go straight back to bed and keep warm." My mother was stirring the porridge on the kitchen stove for the rest of the family's breakfast.

"But I don't want to go back to bed. I want to get dressed," I said, eyeing the silk-frilled dress which hung on a hanger.

"It's half-past seven in the morning – the birds are barely up!"

I spotted the white buckskin shoes with the brown leather heels which we had collected from the shop the day before.

"Can I walk around in my new shoes to get used to them?"

"You cannot. Don't touch anything until you're told. If you get a speck on anything, I'll..." and she stopped.

"I'm hungry." My butterflies were not as fluttery as they had been.

"But you can't have anything to eat." My mother's anxious face peered at me. "It's your First Holy Communion Day. You can have some sips of water and that's all."

Fasting from midnight, that's what the catechism said. It had sounded so grown-up and important when we had learned it all. It was like being a martyr; giving up eating so that we could receive Our Lord in Holy Communion. No food or drink from midnight, and a long fast till after the ten o'clock children's Mass on Sunday, would be the order of the day for the rest of our childhood. Not even a tiny sip of boiled milk in the middle of the night if you had a pain in your stomach, and no sticking your hand in the sugar bowl as you passed it in the mornings. It had all seemed very noble when Sister Genevieve explained it, but now I just felt hungry.

Nonetheless, this day was my day. I was seven years old and today I was the most important person in my family. For one whole day the household would revolve around me. No matter that our mothers carried rain-coats, for us the sky was cloudless as we minced along like little princesses, conscious that people stopped and looked and old women blessed us as we passed. The hunger and the long fast were forgotten as we examined each other's outfits. We compared medals, dresses, prayer books and rosaries and jangled our chain-strapped purses hanging from our white-gloved wrists. We primped in every window and pulled faces and tugged at our tight elastic head-dresses, and got reprimanded by our mothers who stepped smartly behind us; it was a full working day, so there were no fathers in attendance. We were marshalled into the chapel, where three nuns in long outdoor over-dresses darted between us like penguins in a sea of white.

The butterflies were coming back and I looked wildly around for my mother. She waved to me from the porch door. I did not know where she would sit in the chapel. I would be in the third seat from the altar, isolated in the middle of a seat with four of my friends, spaced well apart, on each side. The nuns and teachers swept up and down the long passage between the seats and in loud whispers told us to take off our gloves and join our hands. Then the priest was at the pulpit and it seemed all the altar boys in the world were on the altar. The long candles gleamed in their brass sticks and the Mass began.

I must have been day-dreaming or half-asleep because I was suddenly aware that Sister Genevieve was hissing at me from the end of the seat, and two of my friends were looking over their shoulders at me as they left the pew. Sister Genevieve straightened my veil and whispered in my ear: "Join your hands and keep them joined." I concentrated on making a steeple of my fingers, as butterflies turned somersaults in my stomach. The big moment had arrived. The altar rails were huge. I knelt on the red felt covering and waited, my head barely touching the top of the rail. I couldn't see over it. I could sense a teacher moving along behind me. She tapped me on the shoulder.

"Stand up, put out your tongue and close your eyes."

I squeezed my eyes shut till my eyeballs hurt, fluttered them open for a moment and clamped them shut again. I opened my mouth wide like a gate and flattened my tongue, which wasn't easy. I didn't see the priest coming, because I did not dare open my eyes, but I could smell the heavy cloth of his vestments as he stood before me; then he placed the Sacred Host on my tongue before I had time to be frightened. As I stood, petrified, my shoulder was tapped again. I walked back, head bent over my steepled fingers until I reached my place.

Nothing dreadful had happened. I had not bitten the Host nor had I touched it with my teeth; I had eased it from the roof of my mouth with my tongue and let it rest where I was told it would melt. No little pieces of the Host had fallen on

my hands and I had opened my mouth wide so that the priest
could put the Host squarely on my tongue. If a Host fell on
the ground heaven and earth moved. Nobody but the priest
had authority to pick it up.

We knelt with our heads in our hands in thanksgiving.

"Have you swallowed the Host?" Sister Genevieve spoke to
each child in turn. It took a long time for the Host to melt,
and it stuck again to the roof of my mouth, but the big hurdle was over. There was a lot of whispering as we all sat up to
hear the priest speak: the moment we had prepared for for six
whole months was suddenly, safely past. I looked proudly
around to try to find my mother. I wanted to stand up and
shout to the world that we weren't babies any more.

"I'm starving," I confided to Jennie as we streamed into the
sunshine.

"You can't eat anything until you get home; remember you
have to have a drink of water to wash down any little bits of
the Host before you can put anything else in your mouth,"
she said sanctimoniously.

"I practised it enough times yesterday," I snapped at her. I
was not feeling particularly holy.

I ate my Holy Communion breakfast in solitary state, and
was given my boiled egg the way I liked it best, mashed into a
cup with a big dollop of yellow butter and a dash of salt.
There was still a very important part of the morning to come.
The neighbours had to be shown my grandeur and I had to
be rewarded accordingly.

"Going around like little beggars," is how my mother
described it.

"But I bet you did it too, Mam," I said.

She sighed. She might not like it now because she felt that
many could not afford it, but she hadn't the heart to stop it.
In March, May and December everybody on our road and on

the other roads where we had friends knew to the last child who was for Holy Communion and Confirmation. Shillings, sixpences and thrupenny bits were carefully set aside in a bowl on the sideboard or chiffonier so that when you knocked there was never any question of a mother searching for her purse.

"Don't rattle your handbag," was my mother's parting shot, though she knew the handbag would be rattled for me. Jennie and I made our visits together and as we walked up the small garden paths little children scattered ahead of us to announce our coming. Everything was admired, from the lifting of the dress to see the petticoats underneath to the twirling around to show off the wreath and veil.

"And now, let's see your handbag – oh, but it's heavy." Then the opening of the bag, the slipping in of the coin as I mumbled, "Mammy says you shouldn't do that... thank you very much." And the hand on my shoulder as I walked out the door:

"Tell yer Mammy that it's my pleasure and that you're a credit to her."

The feeling of being special and cossetted filled the day, and the day was not yet over. The luxury of a tram-ride from Dolphin's Barn into Grafton Street to have our photographs taken in Roe McMahon's still lay ahead of us, and there would be cream-buns from Kennedy's bakery for tea. Jennie and I stood at the pole, surrounded by an admiring audience. There would be no pickie-beds today, nor Catch-in-the-Rope.

Then for no apparent reason I stumbled against Jennie and my foot came smartly down on her white buckskin shoe.

"You shouldn't have done that," she shouted.

"I didn't mean it – it was an accident."

"But I've got a big black mark on my shoe," she said. We rubbed at the mark without effect.

"Then I'll stand on your shoe and we'll make it even," said Jennie. Fair was fair. We measured the spot and the size of the mark and she stamped carefully on my foot.

FOURTH CLASS WAS the halfway house of our schooldays, the year when we stood uncertainly, clinging to the images of babyhood and unsure of what was expected of us in the future. This was the year when we were to be made strong and perfect Christians in the eyes of the Church, and emerging young ladies in the eyes of our parents.

Confirmation was frightening.

"They lock you in the chapel for three whole hours and you can't get out, isn't that so?" Kathleen appealed to us, but we couldn't enlighten her.

My two older sisters had been confirmed together, but I would be on my own. We were to be confirmed in the parish of St Catherine in Meath Street. Donore Avenue was only a chapel-of-ease, and it was unheard of for a bishop to come to such a small place.

For months we had prepared, revising the small catechism which we had had as infants and moving on to the big catechism and items selected from the religious knowledge book. In the vast church we would be faced with the ordeal of the bishop's questioning, and if we stumbled in our reply he might not confirm us.

The nuns and the teachers made no secret of their apprehension as the day of Confirmation approached. It was almost as if the good name of the school depended on our answering correctly.

"He'll always ask the child at the end of the row," said Sister Magdalen, running her eye down the Confirmation class.

"It depends on which bishop it is," Sister de Paul said. "They all have different ways of landing on the children. It's

been known for them to skip a row and take somebody un-
awares."

"They'd give ye the jitters with their foosterin' about," I said
to my mother when I arrived home from school, having first
been positioned at the start of a row and then moved to the
middle. "Every one of them is like a hen on a hot griddle. I
wish they'd fizzin' well make up their minds."

My mother had begun to worry, too, but her worry was a
more practical one. Three long hours in a locked church
without a bite to eat: somebody, and it might be her child,
could faint. She had made me a long-sleeved dress of pale
pink satin, with a row of deep hems for letting down and
tucks at the side for letting out. For her first attempt at making a coat, she chose a straight sensible pattern with a fashionable yoke and used dark wine-coloured melton cloth. A felt
upturned-brimmed hat sat primly on my head, with a black
elastic band under the chin anchoring it against the wind.
Sensible shoes, lisle-thread long stockings held up with
garters, and wine-coloured leather gloves completed the outfit.

"And then, when the ceremony's over, girls, you have to take
the pledge." There were no complaints from the girls, but
some of the boys sniggered. Many of them would soon start
to earn pay packets and would be thrown into the tempta-
tions of public-houses and early drinking.

Our school, one of the largest convent schools in the parish,
had a prominent position at the head of the church. We were
marshalled into seats by nervous teachers, sitting well apart
and leaving every second row unoccupied so that the bishop
could squeeze through to shoot a question at somebody in the
middle. As the last lines of "Come, O Creator, Spirit Blest"
died away, I looked up at the high stained-glass windows,
hoping somehow to see the Holy Ghost emerge from the

light. No such thing happened, but the altar brasses shone in the light of a hundred candles, and the candlesticks and cruci-fix, the bishop's throne and the staff which he carried in his hand had a golden glow. There was gold embroidery on his cloak and on the backs of the priests' vestments as they stood facing the sanctuary, saying the opening prayers.

Suddenly I shivered. A watery March sun filtered through the windows and I was cold. The bishop turned to start his examination and there was a great rustling sound as we rose from our knees to face him. He moved towards us, his little court gathered closely about him.

"Sit down, children," he said, "you have a long morning ahead of you." He smiled slowly. As we settled into our seats it seemed as if it was not going to be all that bad; the bishop had a kind voice at least. The first rows on each side remained standing as the figure in the cumbersome vestments moved closer. He walked slowly, speaking now and then to the priests who hovered at his side and saluting the teachers who scuttled from seat to seat ahead of him. He paused every now and then to confront someone with the simplest of catechism questions, while the whole court closed in around the white-faced child; but the bishop had half the answer out before the child even started and he prompted generously if there was any sign of stumbling. Then on, with a nod and a pat on the head.

We turned to watch his progress through the church, our anxious tension receding in his regal wake. I felt cheated. You became a sort of hero if the bishop asked you a question, and I had smiled brightly at him, ready for martyrdom, but he had swept serenely by.

The rest of the ceremony dragged on as each child in turn was brought forward and presented to the bishop, who now sat at the gates of the altar. We were about to change our names. I liked the foreign sound of Thérèse. The name tripped off the tongue nicely, and I had practised signing my copy books with it. When my turn came the bishop placed the Oil of Chrism on my forehead, reciting the Latin prayers while the priest handed him a slip of paper. He leaned forward, called me by the new name, and slapped me gently on the cheek. I was now a strong and perfect Christian. I felt two inches taller as I walked to my place, confident in my new grown-up coat and hat, and bearing my own choice of name.

# Our Daily Bread

THE MONEY AND the shopping bags were always waiting on the kitchen table when we came home from school, and the gas oven would be holding our dinners warm. My mother was always somewhere around, upstairs tidying bedrooms or, more often than not, clipping the hedge, coaxing flowers from our little front garden or whitening the sides of the three front steps with her paintbrush.

"It's your turn for the bread." Madge, Babs and I took it in turns to go for the bread and milk.

"It always seems to be my turn for the bread." I flung my schoolbag into the far corner of the kitchen. It made me tired even to think of walking back past the school again and on to Meath Street to buy bread.

"A ha'penny for a bag of rock," my mother coaxed. Halfpennies for bags of sweets didn't come very often, and the offer might not be repeated if I continued to sulk. I scooped out a nest in the mound of mashed potato and cabbage, put a lump of butter in the hollow, and watched it melt into a pool of golden liquid. I scraped ridges along the potato with my fork and ate carefully around the edge, hoarding and savouring the lake of butter for the last mouthfuls. This delicious dinner and the prospect of a bag of rock to follow filled me with goodwill, and when I had finished eating I picked up the bread-bag and joined Jennie at the playground gate. Our orders were always the same.

"Four fresh loaves, not crusty please," we chanted as we skipped on to Cork Street.

I often tried to visualise what Cork Street must have looked like before I was born. Had I sat down to draw it I would have painted all the old dairy farms surrounding Dolphin's Barn, which my parents often talked about, as the branches of an enormous tree. I knew their names: Lap-John's, White's, Healy's of Towerfield House, Guthrie's, Thornton's, Joyce's, Mooney's fields and Flanagan's. The rhubarb fields which had supplied Millar's, the wine merchants in Thomas Street, I would have put at the top of the tree in red, green and gold. The rhubarb fields were long gone now, of course, and the farms were giving way to new houses.

A blacksmith's forge and an untidy haybarn stood in the present Hollow of the Barn, and then the trunk of my imaginary tree twisted slightly past the tiny whitewashed cottages and little gardens of Dolphin's Barn Street. Rock's forage store stood there, hay piled to the ceiling inside and a four-pronged fork leaning against the wall just inside the open door. Before the tree-trunk straightened in Cork Street there was Johnny Fogarty's shoemaker shop. Johnny was a small tidy man with a short leg, supported by an enormous black leather boot, which he swung expertly as he negotiated his way up and down the street.

"You know you're not supposed to stare." Jennie pushed me along as I slowed in passing.

"I'm not starin'. I'm just wonderin' where he puts it when he wants to sit down." That was something we had never seen him do. In the dimly lit shop he stood close to the little window, catching the last of the fading light, the naked bulb shining on his thin sensitive face as he threaded the waxed ends and hammered at recalcitrant nails.

Groups of shops gathered in clusters so that Cork Street was like a series of little communities. The first part of the street was quiet, with Huxley Crescent sedately set back from the roadway, but at Morrissey's public house and below that at Larkin's we might have to step out of the way of a staggering drunk who would swear if we crossed his path. On the corner of Marrowbone Lane was the Protestant shop. The owner, in his sandy-coloured shop coat, spent a lot of time cleaning the windows and sweeping the street and footpath around the shop. Beside him was the Aughrim dairy, around which cattle lowed and spread dung in crusty-topped cowpats, treacherous to the unwary and probably the reason the shop-keeper had so much sweeping to do. We never gave the hold-ing yard which stood opposite the dairy much attention until during the war years, when the men from the Department closed its gates and put up a big notice proclaiming "Foot and Mouth Disease". Jennie and I carefully edged around the footpath then for fear of catching whatever it was the cows had, but we were reassured by my father that humans, and particularly little girls, were not in any danger.

Next on our way, and leaning drunkenly into one another, were the barber's and another shoemaker's. The barber's shop was uncharted country as we had no brothers and my father preferred to have his hair cut by his old barber in Thomas Street. Beyond that was Lily's dairy. I liked Mrs Lily, as we called her. She was pretty and chatty and, in addition to sell-ing milk, butter and cheese, she had great stores of sweets, and we called it "Lily's sweetshop". We goggled at the great glass jars on the shelf at the back. If we begged the evening papers from home and brought them down to Lily to use as wrapping paper, she gave us a huge bag of sweets in exchange.

Halfway down the street was the great Fever Hospital. We always felt we were entitled to a rest when we came to the Nurses' Home opposite the hospital, so we sat ourselves down on its steps.

"We might get scarlet fever or diphtheria if we sit here too long."

"How?"

"Well, the germs might blow across the street and go down our throats."

"We'll keep our mouths shut while we rest." We stared at the big grey buildings, with the little sentry-box behind the locked gates, and calculated on teasing the porter who came hurrying with arms waving if we went within shouting distance of the gate.

"If we can catch it from sitting here, then what about them?" They were the nurses who bustled across the road, white veils blowing in the breeze, their dark blue and red capes clutched to their breasts when the weather was cold and windy.

A brother of one of our class was in the Fever Hospital with diphtheria. We prayed each morning for him and hoped that his sister wouldn't catch it and pass it on to us. We had seen the green Corporation van outside the house after he had been taken away in an ambulance.

"Every stitch destroyed."

"That's not true, Missus. Ye get the clothes back; they knock the daylights out of them and the germs with the disinfectant in the yard beyond in the Marra'bone Lane."

"God between us and all harm, but it's terrible days we're living in."

"God forbid the fever ever comes knockin' at my door."

"They slake the walls with lime, and they put sticky tape over the bedroom door and nobody's let within an asses roar 'f it."

We knew the disinfectant yard in Marrowbone Lane where they took the bedclothes; it erupted steam, and we ran past, holding our breaths for fear of swallowing any.

Every evening when I looked at the paper to see the Mutt and Jeff cartoon, I was always drawn to the chart headed CORK STREET FEVER HOSPITAL. Each patient had a number and their progress in hospital was reported alongside it. "Slightly Improved" meant that the six weeks of illness was progressing normally, but the dreaded "Not So Well" struck fear into the hearts of families whose only contact with their sick was through the column in the evening papers.

"If we knew John's number we could ask one of the nurses how he was," I said, although the thought of accosting one of the uniformed ones was daunting to say the least.

"They wouldn't tell ye; it's all very secret. None of his family is ever allowed to talk to him," Jennie said knowledgeably. "His Mam puts on a special gown and they only see him through a glass door. If they touched him they would come out in spots."

"Spots," I said disdainfully, "ye don't know what ye're talking about." I was determined to put the record straight. "Spots is chicken-pox; diphtheria is a rash." We gathered our shopping bags together and inspected one another for signs of spots, rashes and inflamed tonsils before going on about our business.

Thursday was cattle-market day on the north side of the Liffey and the cattle purchased for the outlying farms were driven through the city streets, sometimes at a frightening pace. Terror-stricken, frothing, stumbling animals spread across the width of the road, drenching the cobbles and splashing cowpats when the urge drove them. My heart went out to the poor cattle as they stumbled along, and I gave little sympathy to the drovers with their waving sticks. We were never wholly safe when the cattle were coming, and sought shelter in gateways and doorways, but the biggest danger-point was when they approached Donnelly's meat factory which stood below the Fever Hospital on the corner of Brickfield Lane.

I hated Donnelly's; it was a place made from nightmares. But nightmares have a certain fascination and I always stopped to watch the cart-loads of squealing, screeching pigs being unloaded into the dark recesses of the abattoir. I always hoped that a pig would escape when they let down the ramps, but when they did it was never long before they were caught by their struggling hind-legs and hauled back to their bloody ends. From the other side of the street we could sometimes see their lifeless forms hanging on hooks, and the girls from the factory in their red Russian boots, red aprons and white caps moving among the carcasses.

"There's a cow gone amok at the gates of the hospital!"

Donnelly's was always the point where they panicked. The plodding cattle quickened their pace, mooing in distress and agitation, then broke into uncontrolled running. The fright-ened animals sought open space, and lowered their heads to charge anything which stood in their way. Carts were aban-doned and people on the street ran for the safety of the shops. The corner-boys lounging outside the pubs, forever shrugging their heads around corners to see if anything was happening, were suddenly galvanised into life. They came from all quar-ters to shoo the frightened animals until, cornered and trem-bling, they allowed themselves to be led away.

Having taken our rest and negotiated our way past the cat-tle and pigs, most days we ran the rest of the way to the bread shop. Our particular bread shop was on the right-hand side of Meath Street as we turned in from the Coombe. The big mills of Boland's, Kennedy's and Johnston, Mooney and O'Brien had shops solely for the sale of bread, and no thrifty mother worth her salt bought bread for her family anywhere else. Yet fresh bread was something we were not encouraged to eat.

"It'll stick in your guts," we were told, but as I did not know what my guts were, the warning fell on deaf ears.

"Get the afternoon bread; don't let them palm off yesterday's bread on ye." I could never see the logic of it. If fresh bread stuck in your guts, then why buy it? But what I did not realise was that the fresh warm bread bought at four o'clock was just nice for cutting, with no waste about it, the next morning.

Every day in the bread shop was a battlefield. While the privileged few who knew the assistants lounged in the doorway or in the far corner of the shop, most people had to wait outside. When the van containing the manna from heaven was spotted in the street, the crowd swooped on the shop, pushing and shoving and digging with their elbows.

"Let the bread through," went up from the assistant at the counter, was taken up and echoed through the open door to the breadman outside, but nobody moved. The breadman pulled a wooden tray of steaming bread from the van, positioned it at a point above his hips and used it as a battering ram to force his way through the crowd. Not until the war years was there any queuing: the ablest and the strongest got their bread first. As children we had a small advantage. Nobody wanted to hurt a child, so we put our head down, held on to our bags and burrowed between people's legs and arms.

"There's a child below ye, Missus. Here, luv, I'll make a space for ye. Give the child some air." But in spite of our having having made it to the counter, with our heads barely above it, the assistants could ignore our pleading, or try to palm machine bread off on us. Hand-made bread was what we were sent for, though, and hand-made bread was what we brought home, with the threat of being sent back if we didn't. The machine bread was high and slim and had a pale soft crust, while the hand-made bread was squat and bulging, with a hard nutty crust, and it had a hole in the centre where the baker had pressed his thumb before loading the bread into the ovens. The crust responded with a hollow sound when we tapped our knuckles against it. We watched carefully as the shop assistants broke the batches of loaves apart, the pet of the bread swelling as the steam escaped and slowly settling back into position.

My mother placed a lot of trust in our ability to come home with exactly what she ordered. We were often tricked, and the catskin which we were told to avoid could be foisted on us by a seemingly helpful assistant who would slide the four loaves into our bag before we would realise it. The catskin was the shiny outer layer which sometimes had tiny bits of cinders from the oven coals embedded in it. Secretly I liked the rubbery feel of the catskin, but as often as not it was a slice which my mother discarded, and that to her eyes was sheer waste.

We spent the halfpenny my mother had given me at the Ha'penny Bag shop at the end of Meath Street.

"A ha'penny bag of Peggie's leg, please." Manners, said my father, were a light load to carry.

"No Peggie's leg today," the woman behind the counter peered at me; "ye get what ye get in a ha'penny bag. There's no pickin' and choosin'."

"It's all *brus*," I complained to Jennie when we opened the bag outside the shop.

"What d'ye expect for a ha'penny. My mam says it's the sweepin's of the factory floor." Maybe it was, but it had pieces of brown aniseed rock, pink candy-striped rock, broken "glassy" fruit sweets and chunks of Peggie's leg, all of which we crunched between our teeth. Well satisfied with ourselves, we headed for home.

At the bottom of Cork Street was the Ardee Street forge. It was a favourite place for us to stop and rest our tired legs, and anyway I could never pass the forge without being drawn by the gleam of the fire. I liked to stand as close as possible to the patient horses.

"Stay away from them hooves, d'ye hear what I'm after tellin' ye. He'll lash out at ye!" Jennie and I retreated a few paces.

"He's a cranky oul fella," I said. "I wonder does he know at all what he's at?"

"Of course he knows what he's at."

"Well it looks to me as if he's makin' a hough of it. Look at him parin' all that stuff away from the horse's foot."

"He couldn't make a hough of it, or the horse would kick him. He'd a learned it the proper way down the country. That's where all horses come from."

"No, they don't; the city is full of stables. Everything doesn't come from the country." We watched the blacksmith grasp the horse's great shaggy hoof firmly between his knees.

"I hate that smell," Jennie wrinkled her nose as the red-hot shoe was fitted. "I think the whole thing's very cruel." We leaned up against the wall and listened to the zing-zang of the blacksmith's hammer as he teased and coaxed the next shoe into shape.

We could have stayed all day sitting comfortably on our hunkers watching the blacksmith, but the hot bread in our laps was a reminder that we were needed at home. We made one last stop as we passed the toyshop. Its windows were crowded with toys at Christmas, but during the rest of the year it sold everything from a needle to an anchor. We gazed through the glass at a picture of St Thérèse.

"Let's count to one hundred and I betcha she'll appear to us." If she was going to appear to anybody it had to be me; I had just taken her name in Confirmation. We stared at her solemnly. The trick was to stare without blinking for a count of one hundred and then look swiftly up the street.

"I can see her," I whispered. "She's just floating down past the coffin-shop."

"Me, too," Jennie affirmed, "but she's up in the sky. At least that's where I'm lookin' and that's where she should be, if she's a saint."

"She can't be in two places at once; she's not God. Anyway, I don't want to see her. If you see a saint, it means you're going to die." This business of seeing saints walking down Cork Street wasn't appealing any longer. I stamped off.

Coming past the night refuge we quickened our pace. If the women carrying their brown cases and paper bags were gathering outside the door in the convent wall, it was time for us to be home. In wintertime they arrived early and shuffled up and down in the shelter of the convent, or huddled on the far side of the street outside Fry's weaving firm. They did not stand in groups; each woman seemed to hold herself to herself and only crossed the street to the night refuge when the Angelus bell rang, the signal for the door to open.

"The strangest thing about them is that they never really look at people. They make me feel all shivery. What's wrong with them?" I asked my father.

"They're none of your business," he said. I always noticed that questions about them were never encouraged.

"They're poor women who haven't a home to go to, and the nuns look after them," my mother said, busily inspecting the four fresh loaves I had just dumped on the kitchen table.

"I heard tell there's only one room in that building and they all sleep together. Is that true?"

"How would I know?" My father looked at my mother, a look which meant, turn the conversation off if you can.

"It's better than the streets then," my mother said briskly, "and if you'd not dilly-dallied on your way home you would not have seen them, and be standing there asking me silly questions. Your tea's ready; get to it and then do your homework, or you'll end up traipsin' the streets yourself.

"God love them all," I heard her say as I went into the living room, "but it's hard times to be out on the streets, and some of them nearly fallin' out of their standin'."

Bread and milk. Milk and bread. There were at least six shops which sold milk on Dolphin's Barn Street and Cork Street, all within a short distance of our home, but my mother insisted that we buy our milk from a small farm owned by the Joyces and which was known to us as "up the laundry lane". There we could see the cows grazing in the open fields and we got our milk straight from the churns, a penny cheaper than at the shops. Thornton's dairy on the bend of Dolphin's Barn Street had its own farm of fields and cattle grazed at the back of the shop, and occasionally we bought milk from there also. The shop was always cool and spotless, with big earthenware crocks of milk covered with snow-white gauze standing on the wooden counter. A long-handled aluminium measure was hooked on to the edge of the crock. The cover was lifted and the long-handled measure was used to distribute the thick yellow cream, swirling it around until all the liquid was an even creamy texture. When the milk stood in the can at home, the same thick cream settled on the top, and the milk always had to be stirred before pouring.

Third in ranking in my parents' estimation was the railway milk. I was often tempted to go to one of the shops which sold this ordinary milk, which had been transported from the surrounding counties by rail, and see what would happen when I brought it home.

"D'ye think they'd know the differ if we went to one of the shops and brought back shop milk?"

"Mine would. Mam says the railway milk is much thinner than the farm milk."

My father did not trust the railway milk either. "Rattlin' along from early morning in those big churns, and God knows how many days it was standing on the railway station before it was loaded."

We collected the milk in tin sweet-cans. Great care was taken in selecting these cans, which my mother bought in the sweetshop; the joint must be welded strongly and the wire handle safely anchored, and a tight-fitting lid was vital. We had strict instructions to keep the lids on tight to avoid the dust from the streets.

The laundry lane was a narrow dusty track between two high walls which had narrow grassy margins that went wild with pink roses and trailing ivy in summer. It was very dusty in hot weather, and in winter it was treacherous with the mud and wheel-ruts churned up by the carts which drove to and from the laundry halfway up the lane. Beyond the laundry were the fields of Joyce's farm.

Going up or down the lane was an adventure. It could only take the width of a laundry cart, so we would stand at the bottom and calculate if we would make it past the laundry before a cart started out of the yard on its way towards us. Caught in the middle of the lane with our milk cans, we would press back against the wall, hoping that we would not slip into the path of the high stepping horse. The opening to the laundry's yard was forbidden territory for children, but that did not stop us watching as the horses were groomed and their collars and brasses polished; it was their pride and ours that these horses and drays won prizes each year at the Dublin Horse Show.

At the top of the lane stood Joyce's long low rambling farm-house, its front covered in green and gold ivy. Churns of milk, fresh from the morning milking, stood waiting just inside a rose-entwined porch as the cows huddled close to the outhouses waiting for the end of the day. We tapped at the door and an old man with silvery-white hair came out to serve us. Telling us to hold our cans steady, he stopped and burrowed in the churn with his measure, then poured white rivers of milk, sweet and rich, always adding a quick tilly for good measure. Somehow the sky over that farm was always more blue, the clouds whiter there than above our own little roads and streets. Nobody ever shouted at us to leave the farm, so we lingered picking buttercups and daisies to make daisy-chains, and poked our fingers through the wires at the wet noses of the calves. The city seemed so very far away.

To pass the time on our way home we often made a game of whirling our cans of milk in circles around our heads. Starting the whirl was where the skill came in, but once that was mastered you just swung the can higher and higher and as fast as you could go. To whirl the can with a pint in it was easy; you could hear the milk sloshing around. To whirl a can with a full quart and without the lid was a dare not often indulged in.

"Stop it," Jennie shouted at me as I swung the can boast-fully. Too late I realised that a laundry-dray had started up the lane. I pulled in to the side and up on the grassy bank, but my lovely white milk was covered with a grey film of dust. We sat on the grass verge and waited for the dust to settle. We scooped our fingers along the top trying to pick out the specks, praying they would just disappear. We walked home slowly. At our back-gate we parted, and a worried Jennie went home. I lifted the latch on the door and placed the can on the table. My mother came through to the kitchen.

"What kept you?" She looked at me and then at the can. She lifted the lid.

"You were twirling again! How many times have I..." but I was already halfway up the stairs. My sister was sent for fresh milk and I was sent straight to bed, where I lay brooding at the sounds of children playing on the warm evening street.

# Tobacco, Snuff and Chalk

IT WAS HALLOWE'EN and by rights we should have been out knocking on neighbours' doors, gathering apples and nuts for the Hallowe'en party; instead we sat quietly in the scullery while the house filled with friends and relations, the party forgotten.

"Your grandfather's dead, God be good to him." It was my godmother, Lily, who broke the news to us.

"He suffered his own fair share, God knows. A merciful release, Joe," she said to my father as she blew her nose and wound and unwound her handkerchief around her hands. Uncle Johnny had been her favourite man. She would miss his company and his towering strength.

"And a merciful release for ye all, Joe. Peg has been worn out; day and night she's nursed him. Try and get her to sleep now. We'll look after the arrangements."

We sat quietly, hardly knowing what was going on. Every day for months the Jubilee nurses from St Stephen's Green, in their prim navy coats and tight-fitting hats, had been calling to see my grandfather as he lay in his sick-bed. The nurses' black bicycles propped against our front hedge were a constant reminder that Grandfather was dying at the end of a long illness.

The Jubilee nurses went about their work in a quiet unobtrusive way, and never troubled the household. They were sent to my grandfather by the brewery as part of its care for him in his final days. Others cared for him, too, and in the last week we had shared the house with cousins and listened to snippets of conversation as the adults sipped hot mugs of tea and ate ham sandwiches.

"I'm sittin' up tonight, Peg. I'll call ye if there's any change."

"He's failin' fast; God be good to him now, but he can't hold out much longer."

"Ah, but Johnny always had the constitution of a horse."

What was the constitution of a horse? I wondered in those last days before my grandfather died. The tall old man had during his long illness become a shadowy figure, but he had never looked like a horse, of that I was sure.

Grandfather was described as "a fine figure of a man". He was over six feet tall and walked majestically upright, always with his hands clasped behind his back, and often I followed at his heels mimicking his posture. He never seemed to hurry.

My grandfather smelled of chalk and tobacco. His pipe never seemed to leave his mouth, and if it did it sat in one of the ashtrays which my mother left at strategic points around the house. He held flake tobacco in disdain and used Clark's Plug, sold by the ounce, and stored in a special tin box. Taking a piece from the tin, he held it in the palm of his left hand, took his penknife from his pocket and opened it, then slowly and methodically he pared the tobacco into the cup of his hand. With all the time in the world at his disposal, he teased the flakes gently until they were like fine dust and then he shook them into the bowl of his pipe. With a spill taken from a jar on the mantelpiece, he plucked a light from the fire and applied it to the tobacco, slowly puffing and sucking until the pipe glowed red and he covered the bowl with a tin top which had holes in it.

I did not remember his working days in the Guinness brewery. A photograph taken of him on the brewery's "scald bank" showed him wearing a hard hat with a narrow upturned brim which was part of his protective clothing while working. I fingered the hat on occasion and it was as hard as the hob of hell, and no doubt it could resist any thumps or beer casks which might fall on it. He had a long walrus-type moustache but otherwise was cleanshaven and retained most of his hair until the day he died. In winter he wore a soft hat set straight on his forehead and a long frieze great-coat which came nearly to his ankles. His suits, dark grey or black, were always hand-made and worn with a matching waistcoat, from the second-last buttonhole of which was suspended a gold watch and chain. In the last years of his life this was replaced by a silver watch purchased by him in Ganter's Jewellers in George's Street, for the princely sum of £3.7s.6d., and he would show it to us with great pride.

He wore white high-necked winged collars on his shirts and floppy silk ties which he chose with great care. The ties were usually dark blue or maroon, but for special occasions he sported light blue, yellow or white, and in the breast pocket of his jacket he placed a matching silk square, bunched or flowing as the fancy took him.

Grandfather's pockets were a treasure-trove of white pieces of chalk, not only for us but for other children on the road who knew him. Every day without fail he walked to the Band Room in Bridgefoot Street to meet with his cronies from the brewery. The Band Room was their social club, and there my grandfather and the other Guinness pensioners gathered for hours on end, playing "housey" and shove ha'penny. The afternoons were spent at home where he smoked and nodded into gentle dozing, awakened by us as we sought refuge behind his chair from the wrath of my mother.

"What are ye doin' to the childer, Daughter-o?" he would say as he jerked awake and sheltered us. "Sure they're doin' nobody any harm; leave them be." On one or two evenings a week and particularly at weekends, he set off to play cards, or some people might come to our house to set up a card-game. The card-games went on all night, leaving the weary card-sharks to walk home through deserted streets. The stakes were never high; the company and companionship were the attraction. Gathered round a roaring fire, they were content to sip their glasses of porter while the cards in their hands yellowed in the gas-light and the smoke from their many pipes.

The Guinness brewery was my grandfather's life from the day he was accepted as an employee. He passed the initial test of height matching weight, and of bearing strong limbs and weathered hands, with flying colours. He lived in the grey shadow of its great complex until he retired and he never really left its streets until he took to his sick-bed. As a Guinness employee he was entitled to free hospital care, though like most Dubliners he hated hospitals.

"It'd be the quare family that can't look after its own sick and dying..." he would grumble. "Sure ye might as well bury me now. I'd never come out of the hospital alive."

The Guinness brewery had a man of great humanity as their consultant physician, Sir John Lumsden. His services were free to Guinness employees, and the doctor and man in him gave great care and support to the wives and women staff of the brewery. During my grandfather's illness I went with my mother to the red-brick Guinness dispensary in Robert's Street to collect medicines for him. It was bright, airy and filled with white tiles.

"Why can't we come to the dispensary when we're sick?" I asked my mother.

"Because your father doesn't work in the brewery," she said.

"I can't be treated here either, because I have no claim on the brewery since I married your father. They only treat children of workers and staff; they have every attention, be it doctor, nurse or dentist."

I sat comfortably in the waiting-room while my mother went to see one of the doctors, and the matron, her head crowned with a white three-cornered veil, smiled brightly at me through the open door. I spent my time examining the *Punch* cartoons on the walls, little fat, pot-bellied figures which grimaced at me from all corners of the room. I contorted my own face in imitation. There was a lovely aviary on the wall at the side of the dispensary, and the twittering of its many coloured birds filled the air as they pecked and preened and nodded their little heads.

"Why are there two sets of steps?" I asked my mother as we left. She was not certain, but she thought that the right-hand steps were for the clerks, while ours brought us to the door for dependents of manual workers. The manual workers themselves queued outside a further door to see the doctor or the nurse. The brewery made no secret of the hierarchy within, nor of the discrimination between Catholic and Protestant. Catholics, most of them big brawny men from the country or from country families, made up the bulk of the labouring workforce, while the white-collar workers were Protestant. That's how it had been in my grandfather's day anyway, my mother always pointed out to me. Grandfather was proud to work for Guinness's and walked tall in the knowledge that his work gave him not only financial security but a certain status in the community as well. He gave devoted service in his years with the firm, and lived for the welfare of the horses in his care. His concern for horses caused him difficulties more than once during the Black and Tan raids, and he had to walk the streets with caution when a curfew was imposed on the city.

"He didn't see them one night," my mother told me. "Your poor grandfather had his head down when he came into Thomas Court from the brewery stables. He had a sick horse and didn't want to leave it. The curfew had slipped his mind. He walked straight into an ambush at the end of Thomas Court." My mother had been frightened when he had not come home at his usual time and had kept vigil at her window.

"I saw him as he came round the corner. The Tans shouted at him to put his hands above his head. He didn't hear them. I leaned out the window, which was a foolhardy thing to do – I know that now." I could see in her eyes that the memory of that night was still vivid. "I screeched at him and only just in time. The Tan had his gun to his shoulder, ready to shoot him."

Because our grandfather was a Guinness pensioner, we were allowed free Irish dancing lessons at the Guinness Coffee Rooms in Robert's Street. Every Wednesday afternoon we slung our black dancing poms over our shoulders and set off for our lesson. As we walked through the dark brooding streets around the Guinness complex, the clatter of our black chrome-buckled hornpipe shoes echoed off the frowning buildings. My father and mother were aware of the dangers of dimly lit streets on winter evenings and my father always tried to come to meet us on our way home.

"The four of ye stay together. There's safety in numbers. Don't talk to anyone and don't run; whatever ye do, don't run, you could fall and that would be worse." My instinct always was to run; run away from the shadowy corners and uncertain gateways; from the rats scurrying in the dirty channels and the noise of scrawbing cats as they fought at the corners of the grainstore; run until my father's voice hailed us at the corner of Forbes Lane and we danced about him laughing, our feet light with relief.

Madge and Babs were old hands at the Irish dancing game and had won many honours. When I was introduced at the age of five, I progressed from the easy reel to the easy jig, the slip jig and so on, but Miss Essie Connolly, our dancing teacher, despaired of ever making a real dancer out of me. A real dancer could treble her way through the heavy dances, which I could not, and more to the point, I didn't want to. But I was light on my feet and determined to excel in my dancing poms, those light airy-fairy leather foot coverings, so I arched my insteps and pointed my toes and straightened my crooked knees till the bones nearly cracked. I became expert at lead-ins, lead-ups, sliding side steps, toe and heel techniques, rocking on two legs twined together and knee-high jump steps. I began to take honours.

It was the day of the army competition which nearly ended all our dancing careers. A big carnival and fête was being held by the army on the esplanade across the Liffey, and Irish dancing competitions were part of the programme. I was entered for the championship cup competition for the under-sixes. This was a popular age-group; the future stars of the Irish dancing world would be in action, and there was a large entry. My mother spent hours embroidering intricate Celtic designs on the shawl of my dancing costume, but three weeks before the competition disaster befell me. I fell over a neighbour's railing and broke my collar-bone. My right arm was encased in plaster of Paris. My mother withdrew my name. My dancing teacher re-entered it. I danced, with the offending arm in a sling, the sleeve of my costume slit from neck to wrist and flapping in the breeze of the open-air stage. I won.

"Sympathy vote," my father was heard to mutter. Before I could be presented with the cup, however, there was an objection from the mother of the runner-up; then a dramatic announcement:

"The winner has been disqualified. She is over the required age."

I had passed my sixth birthday. The army was thorough and fair in its administration, so my father said, and the rules of the competition were strict. The runner-up was requested to produce her birth certificate, too. She was over age. On the night of my grandfather's waking, the army made its decision, and an army colonel arrived on our doorstep. In his hands he held the silver cup. The first six competitors in order of merit, when asked to produce their birth certificates, had all been over age. The committee had decided in my favour.

But nobody was in any mood for celebrating. The big old man with the drooping moustache lay upstairs in the habit of the Augustinian Order. The tall figure in the dark tweed suit, the winged collar and the flamboyant tie would jig no more for us as we practised our dancing steps. Nobody would step-dance at his wake.

GREAT-AUNT BIDDY, my grandmother's sister, was the last of the old generation. She had joined our grandmother when they left their small farm in County Wicklow and she, too, had settled in the Liberty of St Thomas.

"She did well for herself, Bid did." She was often discussed at family gatherings. When she came up for mention, my ears began to twitch.

"Loaded, she is."

"And why wouldn't she? Not a chick nor child to trouble her and two men under the clay before her. Our Bid is well provided for."

"Ah, but there's nothin' ye could say against her; she's a real lady, if a snooty one, when trouble's about."

"Fair enough, but nobody'll ever put anythin' over on Bid. She's got her head screwed on."

She was tall, like my grandmother in the picture. When we were taken to see her in the house on Summer Street, I watched her every move and fully intended to be like her when I grew up. Our visits were an ordeal for my mother, who issued us with strict instructions before we left.

"Don't touch the ribbon on your head while you're there," she fussed. On a previous visit I had begun picking at the knot in my ribbon, bored of sitting upright on a chair with my legs dangling.

"That child fidgets a lot," Great-aunt Bid remarked. That child, I noted, did not have a name. She called Madge and Babs by their names, but by the time I came along, and then the younger ones, I suppose she got tired remembering. "Does she have St Vitus dance?"

"There's nothing wrong with her, thank you, Aunt Biddy," my mother replied, flashing her eyes at me to behave. "She's perfectly well."

"Then sit up straight on that chair, child, and stop kicking those legs. You'll get dowager's hump." I did not know what dowager's hump was, and I certainly did not like Aunt Biddy's suggestion that mother put a ruler down my back to straighten me. Her back was straight as a ram-rod.

"Oh, Bid was the rare dancer," people said. "A china plate balanced on her head while she danced a jig was no trouble to our Bid."

Despite her unbending manner, I liked her because she was never afraid to say what she thought about anybody. For reasons best known to herself, she kept all her relations at a distance. She stood on ceremony all the time. Her skirts rustled and showed inches of lace above her buttoned boots, and she wore tight-fitting bodices. The collars of her dresses stood high and cupped her head, which was crowned with a wealth of auburn hair, piled high and held in place by fancy combs.

My mother was invited to take tea from tiny china cups, which Aunt Biddy held with three fingers and a thumb, her little finger sticking out, though sometimes she gently crooked it. After a visit to her I would try my best at teatime to imitate the elegant gesture, while sitting bolt upright on a kitchen chair.

Nanny slipped in the back door one afternoon shortly after my grandfather's funeral.

"Bid is gone at last, God be good to her," she whispered, "sure she wasn't the worst," and she blessed herself and we all did the same. My mother, weary still after her father's death, said, "Will I be needed tonight?"

"No, pet, you're not." Nanny's hushed voice spilled little endearments no matter whom she was addressing. "She'll be laid out tonight. Maggie Brunty is with the body now." Mrs Duffy and Mrs Brunty were names we connected with births and deaths, the first to bring the living, the second to wash and prepare the dead for their final journey.

"Has Maggie everything she needs? I have the waking sheets and candles. They're upstairs ready in the box." I knew where they were, too, because I had helped my mother fold the brass candlesticks and the crucifix in paper wrapping after Grandfather's wake.

"Oh, I wouldn't worry yourself," Nanny answered. "You know what Bid was like; she left instructions down to the last T and plenty of money to wake her."

Great-aunt Biddy was waked for two nights. Somebody stayed in the waking-room day and night, because the corpse must never be left on its own. I couldn't understand why. There was never any chance of its getting up and walking out the door, and who in their right mind would want to steal it?

"It's mainly out of respect for the soul that's just departed this life," said my father, blessing himself. "It's so that she won't feel lonely before we put her in the clay. I heard tell there were other reasons down the years, but those days are gone." He didn't think to enlighten me as to what those other reasons were.

My mother and father were duty-bound to take their turn at watching the corpse and their stint could come at any time. Nobody regulated who did what and when, reliefs just took over every few hours as people came and went. Because we were too young to stay home on our own, we were hustled into coats and caps and taken to Aunt Biddy's. The house was packed with people when we arrived. This was a free funeral and Aunt Biddy had stipulated in her will that no money was to be spared on those who turned up to mourn her: they would have free food, free drink and free transport. And they came: there were people on the stairs and the landing, in the little parlour and the kitchen, overflowing into the yard at the back. Hands reached out to pat our heads as we passed up the stairs. Drinking-glasses stood everywhere, on tables, window-sills and beside chairs, and a strong smell of porter and whiskey hung over all.

The waking-room was quiet. There were whispering voices as we were pushed forward to look at the waxen figure in the long brown habit as she lay against the white sheets.

"She didn't change much in death, did she?" one of my cousins whispered to my mother.

"Of course she changed," I wanted to shout at this silly woman. She did not look the least bit like the elegant lady with the proud head and the crooking finger that I remembered. A rosary-beads was threaded through the bony fingers and the haughty face was gentle and empty. I didn't like it and shrank from the bed, but I was urged to dip the long goose feather into the dish of holy-water which lay on a table beside the bed, and sprinkle the dead figure. One of the drops landed on her eyebrow and winked in the flickering light, and I remembered my father's words and wondered if she was lonely. A long wooden coffin with satin lining and big brass handles stood on its end at the side of the bed. Every mirror in the room was covered with black crêpe paper and all the pictures had their faces turned to the wall. The room felt warm and stuffy.

"I want to go out," I whispered urgently to my mother, and she turned to bring me on to the landing.

"Have a pinch of snuff, child; it'll clear your head." I could smell it as I passed, a hot clovey smell which I had sometimes got from Grandfather's clothes. I could see the dusty brownness of it where it had spilled on an old man's jacket; my mother pushed me forward and excused us, and I was spared the mighty sneeze which exploded from the old man.

When I felt better I was allowed to roam up and down the stairs to be coaxed at every hand's turn with biscuits, sandwiches and fizzy lemonade.

"Have a sup of porter; it'll warm the cockles of your heart." My mother was nowhere to be seen so I sipped, gulped, and ran into the backyard where I spat the dark bitter taste into Aunt Biddy's geraniums.

I had never seen so many cheese sandwiches all together in the one place as I did that night. There were whole squares of cheese, and I watched fascinated as unsteady hands sliced knives through their rubbery mass. I bit into a sandwich and gasped for breath as my tongue touched the raw burning taste of mustard, liberally spread. Ham and corned beef sandwiches were offered to the men and boxes of biscuits were spilled in brown, pink and gold confusion on to three-tiered cake-stands. Hunks of dark fruit cake were passed with the whiskey and the porter up and down the stairs.

As the night wore on, all the children were herded into the

bedrooms to rest. I met cousins I had never known and might not meet again until the next funeral. We were tired and full and beginning to whinge.

"Everybody take their shoes off." The command was given in a soft whisper. We were within earshot of the waking-room.

Eight of us piled into one bed that night, and we rolled into one another on the lumpy mattress as we struggled for sleep. There were great brass rails at the top and bottom and brass knobs bigger than the ones on our beds at home. As I nodded off I remembered where I had hidden the big leadener which I had won at marbles the week before – we hid our marbles and sweets in the hidey holes of our brass bed, ready for early nights when we could not sleep and would sneak out of bed to play a quiet game of marbles on the bedroom floor.

The night had a comforting feel about it, and the cold corpse just across the landing wasn't part of our lives any-more. I pushed her to the back of my mind, as I listened to the hushed tones and closed my eyes. I dozed and then wak-ened suddenly: there were raised voices somewhere close. My mother came and bent over us and tucked us in, but the voices kept shouting. Then they stopped; a glass was knocked over and I could hear an angry whisper: "You'll wake the childer; they're all asleep."

"Have ye no respect for the corpse?" Gentle voices urged the angry ones to be quiet. I rose on my elbow and watched as someone in great distress was led out from the waking-room. My father saw me and told me to lie down and every-thing would be all right.

"It's only a bit of a *rí-rá*," he said. "They always happen at funerals." I snuggled down and slept with my father's hand in mine as he sat by the side of the bed.

In the morning we stood like little puppets as we were buttoned into our coats. The grey dawn was creeping over the city as we walked home.

Black stars were put on all our coats for the funeral.

"I'll wear black for three months," my mother said. "That should be enough."

"But you're still in mourning for your father," my father reminded her.

"It's only half-mourning because it's over the six months, and I'll go into deep mourning just for the next three months." My father gave up.

"Why does anybody have to wear black?"

"Out of respect for the dead," my father explained wearily. I had a feeling he was beginning to tire of it. "Full mourning is six or, well, twelve months if you really want to. Then it's half-mourning and – before you ask – that means wearing something white or purple with the black, like a blouse or a scarf. The men wear a black hat, a black tie and they keep the stars on their sleeves for as long as the women keep their mourning."

I pondered it all. It solved one problem for me: I began to realise why women's clothes were so dark and drab. It made sense. Adults died all the time and it was just as well to have dark clothes because they would never go to waste.

Great-aunt Biddy's funeral was done in style. Almost as if she were there to prod us, we sat with straight backs on the plush seats of the big motor coach as the funeral procession wound slowly through the little streets and over the cobblestones until it stopped outside her house. Silently the blinds were drawn on neighbouring houses and shops closed their doors. Respect again, I mused: that word needed thinking about. We paused for a long minute outside the house, which seemed now so deserted and sad. I shivered as I sensed its loneliness.

As we went out the road from the city, the funeral halted again, this time to allow someone to leave word for her family that she had accepted a seat in one of the free coaches. The funeral waited. The drivers leaned up against the cars and the men joined them while we lay back in the luxury of our motor coach. After a time Nanny, my mother and some of her cousins gathered in a group and began chatting. I sighed. It was going to be a very long day.

FOR A SHORT while we imposed on ourselves the task of praying for the dead. We were anxious to carry out the corporal works of mercy, like visiting the sick, praying for the dead and visiting the imprisoned. However, we were never encouraged into anybody's sick-room and we knew no prisoners, so praying seemed the easiest devotion to latch on to. After all, the corpse might not have as many relatives and friends as Grandfather and Great-aunt Biddy. We learned that a white card pinned to a front-door indicated that the deceased had either died in hospital or was only a relative of the household; a white card surrounded by black crêpe and ribbons proclaimed that the corpse was within. After smoothing our dresses and cardigans and running our fingers through our hair to make ourselves tidy, we would knock gently.

"Can we see the corpse?"

"Of course ye can, pet. Come in, come in." Nobody asked if we were friend or foe. Dutifully we approached the bed or the coffin, dropped to our knees, closed our eyes tight and moved our lips in prayer; any prayer would do. Then on to our feet and shake the holy water before glancing around surreptitiously to see if anyone there recognised us. I pondered the large IHS always on the breast of the corpse, whether the habit be white, blue or brown.

"What it means is, 'I have suffered,' and we all have to suffer, so the nuns say." Mary, Maddy, Ann and I looked closely at the corpse. Everybody who died was expected to suffer, and it was only right that they should proclaim it to all and sundry.

"Do you know, I mean has anybody ever told you, what suffering means?" I asked Jennie as we approached the house of a dead person one day.

"No," she said.

"Me neither," I said.

But we visited one corpse too many. One day, having paid our respects to an ancient corpse whom we didn't know from Adam, except that he was an old neighbour, our generous host asked, "Would you children like a drop of lemonade and a biscuit?"

"No, they would not." The sound of my mother's voice froze me even as I had my hand out for the glass. "You," she said, walking in from the hall, "are supposed to be on your way for the messages. Out you go, and make sure you're home before me."

My mother was generous enough to accept our explanation that we were doing a work of mercy, but banned all such visits in future, and any other corporal works of mercy we might have in mind.

"I'm gone off corpses anyway," I told Jennie the next day.

"Me, too. I got a right telling off from my mam. I saw your mam and her giggling together at our door last evening. But corpses is out from now on in."

We transferred our interest in the dead to Mr Smith's two funeral horses which stood outside his door after funerals.

"Do you think they mind the rain?" A sudden May shower had sent us scampering for the shelter of the hedge.

"Their skins are supposed to be waterproof, so they don't really feel anything."

"When the rain's over we'll ask them; my father says horses are intelligent and they understand humans."

"Let's ask them if it's raining in Africa," and we ran across the road where the two magnificent black horses were shaking the rain from their sleek backs, juddering their legs and swishing their manes. Plumes of black and white feathers attached to their leather headbands rose from their heads, and behind them the opulent glass-sided hearse nudged the edge of the pavement, locked in by a big rubber clamp around the wheels.

The horses answered all our questions by nodding their heads once or twice, or lifting their polished hooves and scraping the concrete in a graceful pawing movement. As they solemnly gave their responses, we stood before them convinced that they had second sight. When Mr Smith came out to release them from our enquiries, he carried with him two great fringed covers which he settled over the horses' backs and withers. Then while we stood watching, he climbed on to the driving seat, settled his tall black hat firmly on his head, brushed his neat black suit, and eased the horses in perfect tandem on to the next funeral.

With two deaths in the family, the hooleys which were part of my parents' social life came to a halt. Grandfather had been at the centre of every family hooley, and with his death the heart had gone out of them.

Hooleys were part of Christmas and weddings, but occasionally a few friends and a couple of bottles of porter might start a hooley for no reason at all. People needed to talk and laugh and make music, and friends and cousins we hadn't seen for months would squeeze into our little parlour while the furniture was pushed back against the walls and the floor cleared for the swing of the half-set. We children hung around the parlour door, waiting our turn to be called.

"Order now, order everybody." Somebody had caught sight of us as we hovered. "Let's have a few steps of the hornpipe."

"Make it 'The Garden of Daisies'." This was my father's favourite.

"I'd rather do 'St Patrick's Day'." Madge was the best trebler we had, and she knew what she was best at. My father stood his glass of porter on the floor beside him and diddled a few bars until she was satisfied he had the speed and the rhythm, and then she began. When he tired and his jaws ached, Uncle Paddy, his brother, took it up and they passed the tune from one to the other, while we tapped our feet in time to the music. The dance always finished with a flourish.

"More power to ye, girl, but ye can step it out and no mistake."

"Draw your breath, Joe. Ye'll burst a boiler."

So it went on till my mother decided that enough was enough and banished us to the bedrooms upstairs. In the late hours we crept out and sat on the landing, listening to the hum of voices and the rising laughter, to light tenors taking Kathleen home and the West awakening as the company joined in.

"Noble call now!" And in the silence that ensued while a noble call was passed on, we laid bets as to the identity of the next performer.

"Arrah, ye don't need coaxin'; stop lettin' on your throat's sore."

"Less of the guff outa ye, and get on with the bar of a song. We haven't all night."

We would drift back to our cosy beds as the ones downstairs dozed where they sat and others sang and kept the night going, all waiting together to go in a quiet huddle to the first Mass on Sunday at the grey hour of six o'clock.

# She's Not Dawney

"**Y**OU'RE SOAKING WET." My mother grabbed me by the shoulders and gave me a shake. "Where were you?"

"The nun needed somebody to help her clean up and Jennie and I stayed back to help. I didn't know the rain would be so heavy."

"And of course you took no coat with you. Upstairs this minute and get out of those wet things." My jumper and skirt were soaked right through, and I had begun to shiver. The coal range in the kitchen was lighting and I snuggled up close to it all evening. Next morning my throat was sore, though not enough to keep me from school. Colds were something you caught today and passed on to somebody else tomorrow. You had to be really sick to stay home from school. I was really sick this time.

"I feel all hot and shivery," I said to my mother when I came home at three o'clock. She felt my forehead and looked down my throat.

"Straight up to bed, and if you're not better by morning your Daddy will go for the dispensary doctor." The dispensary was a dull and dingy set of rooms in a red-bricked building in South Earl Street, where you queued on brown benches to see the doctor or sat for hours waiting for the chemist to dispense a cough bottle or a white stomach bottle. My father was sent there next morning at a gallop.

"Tell her she's delirious," my mother impressed on him. I was feverish and my chest had been hurting all night. My mother floated in and out of my vision; she spoke to me, but her voice was swallowed in the mist which floated before my eyes. Soon Dr Toher joined my mother and I closed my eyes while she prodded and poked and stuck a spoon into my mouth to look at my throat. She turned me over on my face and I couldn't have cared if she dumped me on the floor. She thumped my back and listened.

"Pneumonia," she said as she bundled me over again. "It's too late to move her. Get every blanket in the house and cover her. Her temperature is very high. Give her plenty of drinks and I'll be back this evening." To my father she said, "Take this note to the Jubilee nurses. You know where they are."

What a silly doctor, I thought. Of course he knows where they are. They came to look after my grandfather when he was dying and now they are coming to look after me. I must be dying, too. I closed my eyes tiredly, too sick to care.

All that day I faded in and out of dreams and talked, so they told me, all sorts of nonsense. My godmother Lily was sent for. She had always been good to me in a special way, and it was felt that her presence might help to calm me. Through that night and the nights following they sat with me. The Jubilee nurse came; she sponged me and brushed my hair of its tangles and changed my nightdress. The puffed sleeves of her uniform brushed against me and I was irritated. Night followed night for the weary watchers. Word had gone out that I had double pneumonia and the children in school were praying for me each day. I was close to death.

My godmother stood at the foot of my bed with her hand on the brass knob. I rose off my pillow, ordering her out of the room. She moved away, but I repeated that she must *go*, that I did not want her: I hated her. I felt myself moving farther away from everybody; I was above the bed, floating higher and higher, and those in the room below looked to me like little dolls. From somewhere in the far distance I heard my father's voice and footsteps on the stairs...

They told me afterwards that I had been half a minute in the next world. The prompt action of the Jubilee nurse had saved my life. As she rushed up the stairs, she instructed that a bread poultice be made and this she slapped on my chest, turned me over and put another on my back. The poultice raised my temperature and brought on the crisis. I lost consciousness, but the danger was over. I had passed the critical ninth day.

I was coddled and cosseted for months afterwards. Hand-knitted scratchy woollen vests and combinations became regular parts of my everyday clothes. Neighbours shook their heads and referred to me as the dawney one.

"She's not dawney," I heard my mother correct a nosey-parker one day. "She may be thin, but she's quite healthy, thank you." And she intended that I remain that way.

"Down the red lane." She stood over me every morning while I swallowed a concoction of raw egg beaten with a touch of sugar and hot milk.

"I want none of yer andremartins," she would say as we were lined up for our spoonful of cod-liver oil and Parrish's food. We never came willingly, but she would follow the smaller ones as they hid behind chairs and under the table. "This'll put a red neck on you," she told us firmly as we backed away from the threatening spoon. A pint-sized bottle of the vile mixture stood on the sill of the kitchen window, and I eyed it speculatively every time I passed. The lighter cod-liver oil floated like a layer of cream atop the gooey, tomato-coloured Parrish's food. Maybe I could pretend to be shaking the bottle to blend the two substances together, and could just accidentally drop it? But somehow I knew my parents would not be fooled.

When we were sick in bed or in need of succouring from a particularly nasty fall, my father was infinitely gentle with us, and forever reassuring. He was a perfect foil to my mother who grew anxious about every little thing.

"Stop bawlin' your eyes out, you're still livin'," he commanded me as I limped in from the concrete playground. I had fallen while playing Pussy Four Corners, a game we played at speed, running from one corner to another without being caught.

"Close your eyes tight." He perched me up on the kitchen table.

"Hold your hands real tight; squeeze your knuckles," and he scratched the dirt from the grazed knee.

"Keep them closed." He dabbed iodine on, watching to see that my eyes remained closed, and holding me in a big reassuring hug when I began to sniffle. He gave me a rhyme to say.

"Grasp a nettle gently, it will sting you for its pains
But grasp it firmly, full of mettle,
It will soft as silk remain."

Iodine or no iodine, the wound did not heal. The big scab started to fester, and my knee became painful and swollen.

"What's wrong with your leg?" my mother asked me one day as I limped in from school.

"My knee is a bit sore around the scab," I told her. Up on the kitchen table I was hoisted again, my black stocking stripped down and the full damage which I had been concealing exposed. She drew in a short quick breath and I knew I was in for the mother and father of a telling-off.

"Why?" she demanded, "why in the name of all that's good and holy didn't you tell somebody about that?"

"It didn't get bad until yesterday," I said, "when the stocking stuck in it. But I thought it was only the scab coming off." Gingerly she turned the knee around and compared it with the other one.

"Have you a pain anywhere else?"

"It's a bit sore at the top of my leg." I showed her where a little round lump had appeared at the joining of my leg with my body. My mother knew enough home medicine to realise that this could be serious. Within minutes she had ripped up an old sheet to make a bandage and was issuing instructions to Madge as to what had to be done while she was gone. Her coat and hat were on and she hurried around the house, her urgency communicating itself to my sisters. I was installed in the baby's go-car, a pillow supporting my leg from thigh to ankle

"Keep that leg straight out in front of you and don't move it or bend it. Straight out in front of you; we're going to the hospital."

My mother didn't like hospitals and dispensaries and only darkened their doors when there was a very real need.

"Maybe it's only a constitution lump," I ventured as I saw her tight lips and worried eyes. I had heard my father say that "constitution lumps" were harmless.

"It's not a constitution lump; it's septic."

The nearest hospital was the Meath, a good two miles away. She did not stop once on the way. "Thank God, there's no clinic," she said as she wheeled me in the door.

A nurse settled me on a high, hard couch, drew white curtains around me and banished my mother to the waiting area, where she was told to stay. Something cold and wet washed around the scab and I could hear a tinkling of instruments. I closed my eyes tight as a doctor and nurse prodded and pinched my leg, below, above and around the sore spot.

"Aren't you the naughty little girl to go and do that to yourself?" the nurse chided in an effort to distract me from what was going on. I wanted my mother.

"You're not a baby; you're a big girl now. We can look after you."

"But you're not my mother!" I wanted to shout as the tears welled up.

"You're not a baby; big girls don't cry, do they?" And this big girl held back the tears, even though it wasn't easy when they lifted the scab, but they said it had to be done so that they could clean the mess underneath. It stung like mad when they dabbed it with iodine and there were no father's arms about me now, but I told myself again that big girls of eight shouldn't cry.

"It hasn't come to a head yet," the young doctor said. "It's going to take some time." Only boils came to a head, I thought. What did he mean? I didn't ask because I knew that even though I was a big girl of eight years, I wasn't big enough for medical explanations. That was one thing I had in common with my mother; she hated the lack of information and the conspiracy, almost, of silence. The sore on my knee was about the size of a penny. It was raw and red and very, very swollen.

"Keep it open," my mother was told, "until all the pus is out. Bathe it with boiling water; we'll give you boracic powder and bandages. Bring her back."

Morning and afternoon my mother dressed the wound. I dreaded the operation. My mother brought a bowl of boiling water, steam rising from it, to where I was propped up, leg slightly raised on a cushion. She unwound my bandage, rolling it carefully so that it could be re-used. When the end of the bandage stuck to the knee, she dipped boric lint in the boiling water and squeezed drop after drop gently on to the stuck-on covering. When the bandage was safely off, it was time to apply the bread poultice. Boiling water was poured over a slice of white bread and the moist bread placed in a clean piece of sheet, folded over and slapped on the raw knee. For some moments the pain was unbearable, and at first my sisters would have to come to help hold my hands or I would knock the poultice away. As the days passed and the pus was released, the poultices became bearable and my minders could be dispensed with.

The trips to the hospital in the go-cart ceased; the lump in my groin – a new word I had learned in the hospital – disappeared, and a healthy scab formed.

"Let the fresh air to it," my father prescribed one morning. "Let nature do the healing."

Hospitals were avoided as much as possible. They were all right for broken bones and when all other remedies had failed, but my mother resented the long hours she had to spend queuing when she had a home and children to see to. However, I cost her more time in waiting-rooms soon after. Swinging on a neighbour's railing, head first through the bars, left me lying on the ground in an awkward heap, my arm twisted beneath me. My arm was encased in plaster of Paris for six weeks, with regular visits to the hospital to make sure that my fingers were not turning purple or black.

"If they turn green, they have to chop your whole arm off," my schoolfriends assured me, but I brushed that suggestion aside as envy at the fact that I was off written work for all of six weeks.

I always felt that we went to the hospital too early. The doctors never came until they were ready, and if we knew they weren't going to come until noon what was the sense of waiting for them from early morning?

"It doesn't work that way," my mother explained. "The porter closes the waiting-room door at ten o'clock and if you're not in by then, you won't be let in any other way." Some of the porters tried to act like God Almighty, according to one poor woman who hammered in vain at the closed door, but the most dreaded person in every hospital was the Lady Almoner. The Lady Almoner pried into everyone's affairs and sat in judgement on who should and who should not pay for their treatment or make a contribution towards the cost of their medicines. That was her job, and she was hated for it.

My father had great sympathy for hospital doctors. "Worked off their feet," he would say. "I wouldn't have their job for a pension." There was little fear of that. Doctors, nurses and priests were a different people. They stood on pedestals, and we were the ones looking up at them. The doctor made his entrance flanked by students and nurses and preceded by a matron or sister in starched apron and veil who shooed straying children or wandering patients out of the great man's way.

"Sister..." My mother wanted some information.

"Matron," corrected the lady as she swept past. "Sister will be out shortly. If you want something, one of the nurses is the person to ask." There it was: the ladder had many rungs and we stood on the lowest. I registered the fact that Matron wore a half-cape of blue and her head-dress was different, and during my remaining visits I spent my time trying to work out how the hospital's ranks were coded. It kept me occupied, and beat counting tiles on the walls, squares on the floor, bars on the radiators and feathers in women's hats, the last getting me into a lot of trouble as I walked among the waiting queues, and earning me sharp words from my mother. She never wasted a minute of her time; the thought was foreign to her. She carried her bag of knitting everywhere, clicking and clacking her way through plain and purl, cast-on and cast-off and slip-stitching; she measured and marked, chatting and exchanging knitting know-how if the mood took her and the company was congenial.

"Stay away from the doctors and stay away from the hospitals," was my father's advice. Nobody worried about colds too much; dripping noses and racking coughs were taken to school, and measles got short shrift.

"Don't coddle them; you have them cloustered. Harden them up a bit," my father would say when one or other of us was kept home from school. It was he, however, who rose in the middle of the night when somebody had a tummy-ache. He would slip down to the kitchen and boil a mug of milk, sprinkle it liberally with pepper and make sure the sufferer sipped every last drop. It was he who talked us to sleep and twisted his hands to make rabbits' ears on the bedroom wall when the streetlamps outside threw sinister shadows and nightmares made us cry out in distress.

On the whole, minor ailments such as colds, sneezes and 'flu were dealt with smartly and hadn't a hope in heaven or hell of surviving the fumes of warmed Vick's Vapour Rub, vigorously massaged on chest and back. Hot freshly squeezed lemon-juice, sweet with sugar and laced with a little whiskey or brandy, sipped in a bed warmed by an enormous earthenware jar, made it almost worthwhile to have a streaming red nose and prickly sore throat.

Old-fashioned cures were handed down from grandparents and shared between neighbour. There was a solution for every complaint.

"The barley water, Ma'am, for the low back and the kidneys. It couldn't be bet."

"Ye can't beat the mouthful of cloves for the toothache, and where would ye be goin' without the sheep's wool for the earache," which we faithfully gathered from the blackberry bushes on the Crumlin Road.

"Strain the tea leaves, Daughter-o, and bathe the child's eye with it. The 'flamation'll go down in jig-time, mind what I tell ye." But to my mother the stye in a child's eye was a warning sign that all was not well.

"She needs a good tonic, and I know just the thing." She handed me the money. "Go to Egan's in the Barn and get me a half-pound of good stewing steak." I didn't like this sort of shopping. My mother's idea of good lean stewing steak and the butcher's did not always coincide, and it was quite likely that I would be sent back if what I got was not good enough.

"Half a pound of lean stewing steak," I piped up to the butcher.

"Shin or rib?" I was stuck. "What does she want it for?"

"Well..." I said, "well, my sister has a stye in her eye. My Mam says the cold tea won't make it better, and she says she knows just the thing for it."

"Oh, then she'll need a piece to put on the eye to draw out the stye," he said, surveying the pieces in front of him on the wooden block. "This should do it," and he parcelled the piece of steak up carefully.

"Take it back this minnit," my mother said when she had inspected my purchase. "The cheek of him. I want that meat to make beef-tea for your sister; and I mean good strong beef-tea. If he hasn't got better nor that in his butcher's shop, then tell him I want my money back."

When Mother needed something, we were her staff, running errands.

"Run to the chemist and get me tuppence worth of glycerine and Hippo wine and squills. It'll loosen the chest." My mother put great store by this syrupy mixture.

"It's wine from a place called Hippo," the chemist explained in answer to my questions. "The squills is a herb – a bulb – and good for your innards." I nodded gravely in response.

LIKE ALL DUBLIN people, my mother was also a great believer in the power of St Blaise to cure sore throats.

The Feast of St Blaise, the third of February, was honoured in Adam and Eve's, the Franciscan church in Merchants' Quay, and every Dublin family, north and south of the Liffey, made its way there for the blessing of the throats. For our part we would walk the two miles there and two miles back home again.

"Is the queue long?" my mother would ask of those making their way home.

"Middlin' to long; to the top of Winetavern Street Hill and up Cook Street on the other side. But they're millin' around the chapel door."

"Hurry, for God's sake, childer; we'll be kept all day."

We joined the crowd of people streaming past the stalls which had been set up all along Thomas Street and High Street.

"Get yer oil and flannel here," the dealers called. "Tuppence for the bottle 'f olive oil; genuine olive oil and the best of woollen flannel – that'd roast the neck 'f ye. Have it blessed by the priest and I'll guarantee ne'er another sore throat. Look, Missus, I'll give ye the lot for sixpence." The stalls were bedecked with squares of red flannel, which the sufferer wore around the neck, and there were pictures and medals of the illustrious saint. My mother was used to the palaver, and knew that the goods on the stalls were probably three times the price she had paid for hers, and which she had safely stored in the foot of the go-cart.

The queue shuffled down Winetavern Street, on to the Quays and the doors of the Franciscan church. Resplendent in their semi-monastic garb, the men of the Third Order – a sodality for men and women run by the friars – marshalled us into lines of four. Prams and go-carts were left outside, safe in the precincts of the church, and the patient stream of men, women, children and babies pushed to the altar rails. We stood while a priest cradled two candles cross-wise about our necks, blessed us and prayed the prayer of healing. Our belief in this ceremony had been fashioned over generations. On this day the bearded saint, who had cured a young boy whose throat had been pierced by a fishbone, was beseeched, implored, bribed and glorified. As spring followed winter, so the Feast of St Blaise followed Christmas, our first spring outing and a promise that winter was over.

On the way home I looked at the dealers on the stalls, huddled in their great woollen shawls against the nippy February air. There seemed to be a certain age when some women decided they would discard coats and take to the shawl. The fall of the shawl depended on the person who wore it. It could give dignity and a certain grace to some, but most women wrapped in shawls seemed to have their heads down as they hurried along, the shawl held tightly over head and breast to prevent it slipping. There never seemed to be a brooch or a pin to keep it in place.

Black loosely woven shawls were worn for weekdays; plain black woollen cloth with the material bobbed on every edge. Beautiful patterned light brown shawls, "paisley-pattern" ones with elegant fringing or black intricately self-patterned ones were reserved for Sundays and holy days. On weekdays the shawl could hide the things that needed concealing, like the jug of porter or the baby suckling at its mother's breast.

"If'n we wore a shawl we wouldn't have to wear a hat for Mass on Sundays." No girl or woman was allowed inside the church without some covering on her head.

"The nuns wear shawls, and Our Lady wears a shawl in all her pictures and her statues."

"But it's more like a cloak with Our Lady."

"Don't be crabby; it's a shawl."

"How does she keep it on her head so that it doesn't fall off?" We considered the question with the seriousness a religious matter required.

"I know," Jennie said, "it's a miracle."

"Don't be stupid," I said. "She was painted that way before the shawl fell off."

MY PARENTS INVOKED the intervention of saints on my behalf more than once: I was accident-prone or so I was told. I did manage to have more things happen to me than did Madge or Babs, but I couldn't help being adventurous. When I broke my collar-bone the second time, mother decided it was time to visit the grave of Father Charles in Mount Argus. She had heard that he was particularly sympathetic to the plight of mothers who had over-active children; he protected, so she was told, those who fell out of cots, into fires, off lorries or under horses' hooves. I objected strongly as I trudged beside my father along the canal and up the hill by Mount Jerome cemetery, to kneel at Father Charles's grave.

"If Father Charles makes my collar-bone better, I'll never know, will I?" Father raised his eyebrows at my reasoning.

"If we keep the plaster on my arm for six weeks, that's a long time to wait to see if Father Charles has cured it. Hadn't we better take it off?"

"You're right, ye know," my father said wearily. "But it's not your arm we're worried about, it's your head. It might be that the next time. If he makes ye stay easy and keeps ye out of trouble from this out, then my prayers will be answered. We're only asking him to give ye sense. God knows, it's not too much to ask."

When I got home my mother told me I was going to have to repeat the journey every day for the next nine days. She did not believe in doing anything by halves, least of all when it came to schooling her daughter's wilful energy.

We heard of priests around the country who, by laying hands on sick people's heads and praying over them, could cure them from diseases which had resisted the normal medical treatment. When my sister had been slow in recovering from whooping cough, we were all bundled into coats and taken to John's Lane church on Thomas Street to see Dr Walshe, an old Augustinian priest who was reputed to have "the cure".

"I don't have whooping cough; why do I have to go?"

"Because you'll get the blessing and you'll feel the good of it."

"Is he a real doctor?" I couldn't understand how he could be both a priest and a doctor.

"Maybe he was before he became a priest. In any ways he's a priest now, and that's what matters." My mother believed with all her faith that this old priest might end the whooping cough which had plagued Nance for weeks. The doctor had warned my mother that the disease was rampant in the city.

"Every house has somebody with it. Keep her in bed and warm for a week or so, but it has to take its course." The doctor prescribed a cough-bottle and we all took turns in keeping Nance company and holding her tightly when a spasm of coughing gripped her. It was distressing for my mother and father. The characteristic whoop which accompanied the gasping for breath could be heard on buses, in churches and on the streets, and frightened mothers hurried their little ones home in fear of their getting infected. I had played my part in the fight against the whooping cough, too.

"They're spreading tar in Cork Street." My mother's tone was urgent as she hurried in from shopping. "They're doin' the street in dribs and drabs and they've just opened up the Nurses' Home." She was bundling Nance into her coat and hat and scarf.

"Get down there before they close up. Stand her near the machine when she coughs." The haste with which we went down Cork Street had Nance spluttering and coughing when we got to where they were spreading the hot lava-like tar. I held her close to the bubbling, sulphurous mess and thumped her as directed, but it did no good, so here we were at the Augustinian church searching for another cure. The queue stretched out from the church door and around the corner of the street.

"He's very crochety," a woman with a small boy nodded at my mother. "We'll be lucky if we get to see him. He stopped the blessings early last Sunday."

"I believe he's in his nineties. I believe he's not very well at all."

"It's a wonder he doesn't cure himself," I muttered to Betty. My mother had sharp ears.

"What are ye huggerin' and cumuggerin' about?" she said, separating the two of us.

"Have ye ever seen him before?" an old woman asked my mother.

"I've never clapped eyes on him in me life."

"Oh, but he does wonders with his saintly hands. There was a woman here last week and she came back just to tell him she was cured. She had a big ulcer on her ankle and all the ointments the doctors and the hospital gev her, she might as well have thrown them in the Liffey. Himself put his hands on the ulcer and she's never looked back since."

We listened to this story as we shuffled forward. My mother had begun to realise that my sister's ailment was nothing compared to the stories circulating around us. We were healthy, young, well-cared for and had no twisted limbs among us, but there were children here who had, as well as old people with swollen legs and ankles and pale-faced young men and women, coughing their hearts out.

This wasn't a friendly queue; it was sad and burdensome. Mother gathered us tightly round her and told us to face forward and to stop our gawking. I knew from her manner that she was uneasy. From the time we were toddlers our parents had instilled in us a concern and regard for those who were not as fortunate as us.

"You never laugh or jeer at somebody less well off than yourself" was impressed on us at home and in school.

"My mam says that if you do, then God might strike ye dead," Maddy once announced dramatically. The prospect of God striking me down occupied my mind for a long time and renewed itself whenever I passed a maimed person be he young or old, so that I was very quick with my blessing. "God bless the mark," became an automatic chant.

When our turn came, Mother pushed us into the small room where the priest sat. He put his hands on each one of us in turn, but lingered over Nance as she clung to my mother. His frail hands held her head and slowly he traced the sign of the cross.

We made our way back past the queue, which hardly seemed to have diminished, and one remark stood out in the hum of conversation.

"When all fruit fails, Missus, we always come back to the prayer."

On the way back from John's Lane we stopped at the watchman's hut at the corner of Rainsford Street. As I watched the heat shimmering on the red embers of the coke brazier, strangely I shivered as I remembered the scene we had left behind. I glanced at my mother as she allowed us warm our gloved hands and help the watchman position his lantern for the night. She looked tired, and I sensed that she, too, was remembering the hunched people in old Dr Walshe's queue. I knew that she would guard our health and welfare in every way she could, whether by prayer or pilgrimage, hospitals or doctors, or well-tested local cures. The certainty of her care gave me a feeling as warm as the hot coals heaped on the watchman's fire, and I held her hand tightly as we turned for home.

# The Busiest Day of the Week

SATURDAY WAS A day for cleansing and purging the body and soul. It started with senna tea.

"Here's a nice cup a tea before I go out to the shops."

The smell preceded my mother up the stairs. By the time she crossed the bedroom door, my head was under the bed-clothes, but there was absolutely no way round it. Each family had its own rituals, and one of ours was senna tea. It was no different for any of my friends, some of whom had castor oil to contend with. Castor oil, according to the know-alls, was good for everything: it cured colds, fevers, 'flus, tummy-upsets and pains in the head.

"It clears the system," I overheard a woman say expansively.

"What's the system?" I asked my mother.

"You were ear-wiggin' again," she said, "to things that should be no concern of yours."

My mother was up and about from early morning, for Saturday was the busiest day of the week. She liked us to stay in bed a little late, to give her a chance to get her day started without having us under her feet.

"I'll be about an hour," she said as she was about to leave. "Get the younger ones up, and make sure you all walk on the newspapers downstairs; I've scrubbed the floors and I want to polish. Be good," she called as she went out the door.

The squares of newspapers were like islands on the floor, and we hopped from one to the next. Later in the morning my mother would take her kneeling pad and spread Mansion floor polish over the living-room floor, then she would take a soft rag and polish the wood till it shone. We helped as we got older.

She had hardly gone when she reappeared.

"I forgot: somebody start on the brasses. And don't make a muck of the paint on the front door."

The front door must gleam for Sunday morning. The number, letter-box and keyhole got their weekly dose of Brasso and never a stim must show on the paint-work of the door. The long brass rods on the stairs creaked as we unlatched them and laid them on newspapers on the kitchen table for their weekly cleaning. Each rod was turned over, smeared with the yellow liquid, allowed to cake to a flaky whiteness and then polished with a piece of old flannelette nightwear. Our fingers turned green and then black, and we returned each rod to its place gingerly, careful that no sweaty thumb-marks stained its pristine glory.

My mother's trip on Saturday morning was to buy meat for Sunday's dinner, a responsibility which was never entrusted to us. For the weekends she favoured boiled meats, bacon or corned beef, the corned beef cooked after steeping it overnight to draw out any excess salt. It was economical if it was served cold and there was always some to spare for Monday. Lap of mutton made white Irish stew during the week, with flour dumplings to fill it out. Then a Wicklow rabbit made tasty soup and the tender meat made Thursday's dinner something special. Beef-tea simmered all year round, and supplemented the potatoes, turnips and cabbage which were our principal vegetables. Herrings, with the backbone yanked out and the creamy white pay still inside, made crispy eating on Fridays.

I hated butchers' shops and was glad that my mother did not need company on her Saturday morning rounds. Butchers' shops were bloody places; blood congealed on the chopping blocks and was streaked down the fronts of the men's aprons. Lumps of corned beef and brisket sloshed around in earthenware troughs, watched by rows of pigs' cheeks, pressing together jowl to jowl against the glass counters, while beef sausages hung from the ceiling alongside sticky yellow flypaper.

Seezer's the pork butchers in Dolphin's Barn Street was hospital clean compared with the raw brutality of the beef butchers. The shop was cool, the sawdust on the floor clean and dry, and the assistants seemed perpetually poised to wipe any speck of dust from the glass shelves. Rolls and oblongs of cooked meats were displayed on white marble slabs, and the chubby head of a china pig glowed with contentment, belying the screeching we heard regularly from Donnelly's pig factory.

"Do ye think she'll stop at the Scotch shop?"

I was sitting on my heels on the kitchen floor, reading the cartoons in the evening papers, Mutt and Jeff and Mandrake the Magician, and following the antics of Fay Sargent's Mrs Casey, Mrs Burren and Mrs Win-the-War. My mother was late coming back, and we hoped against hope that it was the Scotch shop which was the cause of her delay.

Mrs Stewart's shop was wedged in the corner of Dolphin's Barn Street. Hot baking smells wafted from its open door: of hot coconut slices, moist with raspberry jam; dark fruit-filled slabs of gur-cake, topped with coconut and edged with pastry; the fresh aroma of milk break, crispy and brown; sultana soda-bread, butterfly cream buns and almond paste. Sugar-covered cream horns oozing jam held pride of place beside the cauliflower cakes. I would press my nose against the window to marvel at these creations. A vivid green almond paste formed the outside leaves of the cauliflower while the centre was a carefully piped mass of creamy flowerets. We never had a cauliflower cake, because they were so expensive, but Mother would sometimes bring home coconut or fruit slices. Their sweet, fruity smell would fill the room as she lifted the latch on the kitchen door, and six willing slaves were in the kitchen before she had placed her bag on the table.

In the ritual of preparations for Sunday came the cleansing of the outer body. If senna tea was meant to take care of the inner woman, we relied on Lux soap-flakes to clean the week's dirt from our bodies.

"Oldest first." My mother, her sleeves rolled up, set the basin of sudsy water on the kitchen chair. She took each of us in turn, pummelling our heads and scrubbing briskly with a flannel. Madge, Babs and I could nearly manage on our own but had to be helped to complete the task. Mother filled jugs of cold water from the kitchen sink and poured it relentlessly over our heads as we gasped and spluttered beneath the icy onslaught.

"Hold your nose and forget about your ears. They won't fall off."

"They're full 'f water and I can't hear," I cried as I came up for air. My mother and I had had a running battle about ears ever since Nancy Dunne told me that if I burst the drum of my ear I would die. I did not know what the drum of my ear was, and in sensible moments I knew that Nancy Dunne did not either, but I was not taking any risks

"I'll give ye Nancy Dunne," my mother snorted as I clapped my hands over my ears and refused to have them dried. "You'll have my good kitchen floor possin' wet with your andremartins," and she wedged me on to a kitchen chair and dried my head till the scalp tingled and my ears were glowing hot.

Saturday progressed as had been ordained for my mother and father and their families before them, and if the old order should ever changeth, it would not be in our childhood. Of that we could be certain.

Confession, our weekly purging of the soul, came next. With wet hair streaming in the wind in summer or well covered up in winter, we presented a solid front at the Confessions for children in Dolphin's Barn chapel. It was the nearest chapel and there was still much to be done in the hours that were left to Saturday.

"Children will be heard on Saturday mornings; the evenings are for grown-ups."

"Yes, Father," we chorused. And "Yes, Father" was what I said meekly when I presented myself for the evening Confession one Saturday. I was there at six o'clock in order to be first in the queue.

"Don't you know you should have been here this morning, child?" The priest's glasses glinted dangerously at me through the grille.

"I had to mind the baby, Father. She was sick and Mammy was doing the shopping and my sisters..." I stumbled over my explanation.

"Evenings are the time for the big people's Confessions. How long since your last Confession?"

"A week on Thursday."

"Well, hurry up then."

I proceeded with my spiel of sins while he peered out at the crowded seats in the chapel. When I was finished I tip-toed out, feeling more guilty than I had going in, knowing as I looked at the bowed heads outside each of the four

Confession boxes that in some way I was trespassing.

With the most expensive purchase of the weekend safely stored under a muslin cover in the tin meat safe in the kitchen, my mother concentrated on her list of groceries and vegetables. She considered that anybody who took looking after a family seriously shopped where the range and quality was best, and, besides, the tuppences and thruppences she saved on every item were better in her pocket than in the shopkeepers.

That was when the question of the box-cart came up. With so many sacks of vegetables to take home, our small arms needed some help.

"Can't we take the inside out of the pram and use it like the dealers do?" I suggested. The pram was no longer in use and stood forlornly in the garden shed. The idea made sense, I thought, but my mother turned her eyes to heaven.

"What we need," she said, "is a box-cart."

There was plenty of wood in the shed, and my father arrived home in triumph one day from the Daisy market, carrying a set of wheels. The making of the oblong box was easy work for him and he attached two long wooden handles to the sides for pushing or pulling, as the mood took us. We painted it a Corporation green, a dull Nile green which was used on lamp-posts, pillar boxes and the new double-decker buses. That box-cart quickly found its place in the family. It was trundled out in the afternoons when we came home from school and became a pram for our dolls as we played "mothers"; in grander flights of imagination we turned it into a carriage with ropes tied to its handles and slipped over somebody's shoulders. However, it was as a conveyor of vegetables, fruit and groceries on Saturdays that it came into its own.

"It's not bucketin'," my mother said one wet windy

Saturday. "You'll be well protected in your raincoats." Those raincoats were the bane of my life. They were made of a rubbery oil-cloth material and had matching rain-hats which dripped water down the backs of our necks. We pushed our feet into heavy rubber boots which came to our knees and which froze the toes off us.

"You thank God you've something on your feet on a day like this," she said in reply to my grumbling. "You'll meet some today that won't."

It was not long before we did. At the bottom of Cork Street we could take a short-cut to the Coombe through a narrow lane with tenements on one side. As we pulled the box-cart over the cobbles we saw babies with shifts hanging loosely on them, their bare bottoms blue with cold. Boys and girls ran about barefoot, splashing in the muddy channel which flowed down one side of the lane, and then they disappeared whooping into the dark halls of the tenements. A peculiar scented smell from the Rice Steele Chemical factory at the end of the lane hung in the dank air. As we came nearer town, skinny little paper-boys, with sacks around their shoulders and tricorne hats made from brown paper on their heads, yelled "Herald or Mail" from the doors of pubs. Poor children were part of everyday life, though we edged away from their cold, raw figures as they stood beside us in the shops. Just as we expected to have shoes on our feet, so they expected to have none, and the shoes that were given to them by nuns from the various convents disappeared as quickly as they had come, pawned or sold to pay for more essential things. It was none of our business to comment or pity, and they would not have thanked us for either.

On Saturday the shops bulged with produce and goodwill to all men, and particularly women. Crates and cartons claimed unlawful space from the footpaths while the stallholders stood brazenly, beckoning would-be customers and jingling their apron pockets in strident encouragement. Here was the date shop where slabs of matted dates stood with a wicked-looking knife embedded and poised to slice the fruit into sizeable portions. When my imagination was high, I could nearly see the heel-marks of the people in Africa who had, my father said, stamped the dates into the boxes with their feet. There was Emmy O'Neill's where we could buy skinny little rabbits with their grey-furred heads and bobtails still intact. The glorious colours of fruits we could never afford spilled from Maisie Hannigan's stall, bringing sunshine to the street even on a wet and dreary day.

"No stops on the way and don't dawdle. Go straight to Jack Roche's. The fresh vegetables may be gone if you're not early." We treated my mother's order with the sceptism we felt it deserved, for Jack Roche always had plenty of vegetables. They spilled from his cart on to the street: dark leaves of York cabbage cradling small white sweet hearts, the crinkly Savoy, yellow turnips and huge golden-skinned Spanish onions, long-tailed white parsnips. Jack's horse, loosed from the shafts of the cart, munched contentedly at whatever fell within reach, while his owner advertised his wares, punching the air as he spoke.

"If ye don't like the cabbage, Ma'am, there's plenty who will, so I'll thank ye to leave your hands off it."

"What ails ye, Jack? You've a face on ye like a wet weekend."

"And so would you if ye were in the muck and slush 'f the market since sunrise and then have to face the sour pusses of you lot."

"I declare to God, Jack, but them cabbages are only babbies."

"I hadn't much to do with the rearin' 'f them. Two for the price 'f one then, and that's the bargain of the week. Try gettin' that from the dealers in Thomas Street."

Jack had a smile and a sharp-witted answer for everything that was thrown at him. With us, he listened attentively to our shopping list and never brushed us aside as mere children. He sold with a lavish hand, jingling half-crowns, shillings and sixpences, pennies, halfpennies and farthings in his big money pouch to make our change.

From Jack's, we pushed the box-cart up Meath Street and into Thomas Street. On we trudged to Kennedy's Mills where we bought flour for my mother's apple cake and scones, and for cookery lessons in school. The mill was cool and quiet, a grey, cobwebbed world, and little white moths danced in the sunlight when we pushed the street door open. I could close my eyes and think I was in a cave, and the lady assistants were little grey mice scurrying among the sacks.

"Why do they all have grey hair?"

"Don't be silly. It's the flour."

"But they look the same, as if they've just come through a mist."

"Don't let your imagination run away with ye."

Still I wondered what lay in the burrows of the store, behind the grey sacks piled at every corner and the brown and white mountains of flour. When no one was looking I liked to run my hands through the bran, the lentils, the split peas and the beans, and if a silver scoop was left in the flour I banked it into heaps and delved my hands into its starchy texture. I was in a muffled world of my own, the dusty sour smell of the mill flat and damp and strangely soothing.

We were on the last leg of our journey. Along Thomas Street we negotiated our way around the heaps of vegetables, past horses munching deep in bags of hay and giving off the hot steamy smell of urine, and the tail ends of carts standing in our path.

"There he goes – somebody catch him."

"Where?"

"Leggin' it up the street, like all the divils in hell were after him." His bare feet had made no sound when he darted in and out pinching an apple there and an orange here, but his progress now was marked by angry shouts. I had a secret admiration for these barefooted urchins who seemed to care for nothing and cheerfully accepted a clout across the head if somebody stretched out a hand as they ran and caught them by the shoulder of their torn jackets.

"Look at me apples; look what he's gone and done!" A carefully constructed pyramid of apples and oranges had come crashing down on the footpath. Nobody made to catch the culprit, for they were more interested in picking the apples and oranges rolling on the pavement.

"He's only a chisseler, Ma'am," a woman offered by way of consolation.

The dealer drew her shawl tightly round her shoulders and glared at the woman who had spoken.

"Ye have me there, Ma'am," she said with heavy sarcasm. "Mary-Ann, did ye hear what the woman just said: 'He's only a chisseler.' Tell her, Mary-Ann, how I've been to the market since six o'clock this mornin' – while ye were abed, Ma'am – and as God is my witness it took me the best part 'f three hours to fix them apples on me stall. If I lay me hands on that varmint..."

We pulled the box-cart away and continued up the street, each of us eating an apple from our own load. We turned into Thomas Court, and there the young thief was.

"Butts on ye!" he yelled and he swiped the apple from Betty's hand.

On most Saturday afternoons my father gathered his tools and materials and sat at the long bench in the kitchen, whistling through shut teeth as he lined them up around him. There were off-cuts of leather which he had bought that morning, protectors in curved angles of rubber or steel, hundreds of tiny bluey-black bradnails piled in the corner of his narrow tool-box, and his heavy three-sided iron last.

"Another pair for heeling. Tell me child, what do ye do with your shoes?

"Ye've scuffed the toe 'f that shoe again; if ye don't stop the climbin' ye'll not have a shoe to your foot, and ye can go barefoot.

"Didn't I tell ye to say when the sole goes soft; it means it needs mendin'; what's the use of it when there's a great big hole in the sole; it gives me twice the work."

None of his comments were meant to be answered: they were just a prelude to the business of shoe-mending. With six pairs of active feet to be shod, he was kept fairly busy.

Muttering under his breath about the quality of the leather, the state of the country and the state of the footwear in his hand, he balanced the shoe in front of him and carefully assessed it. Then he chose a piece of leather, selected for size, thickness and weight, and with a black lead pencil he marked out the shape of the sole or heel required.

"Stay out of my way and if you want to help, get me a basin of water and put it on the kitchen chair there."

Very roughly he cut the leather to the approximate size; he did this for all the shoes to be mended that day. The rough shapes were left to soak for an hour or more in the basin of cold water while he put heel tips or steel toe-pieces on the other shoes needing attention.

"It does two things," he said one day in answer to my question. "It softens the leather, so that I can bend it to the shape I want it." Shoe leather was hard and unyielding to the touch. "And it swells the leather, so that when it dries on the sole of the shoe it tightens the fibres; the leather becomes hard as it dries and no more water will get through the sole."

Putting a sole on a shoe gave him great satisfaction; there was something to show for it at the end of the day. Slowly he prised the old sole off, cutting it back where it joined the arch; then he sprang the tacks out in one or two fast movements, and sat back to tackle the job. A piece of leather was offered to the shoe and looked at from all angles, then cut to the exact size and pared back so that it graduated away from the side. The shoe was slipped on the last to tack the sole. This was tricky: no bulges were allowed to appear as he worked. A tack at the toe and then stretch the leather to the middle; one tack at either side and he was ready to go. He filled his mouth with blue tacks and swung into a rhythm, hammering swiftly until one hit a stubborn spot and he damned it to hell. But his fingers were sure and he spaced the little blue tacks in neat rows, smoothing out any little bulges that appeared.

Sitting up straight he pulled the shoe off the last and reached for his sacred leather-knife. If I was watching I did not speak now; this was the most dangerous part of the operation. This knife was kept well honed and far out of the reach of any childish hands, and it was used only for leather work. He slid backward along the wooden bench, swung one leg over and gripped the shoe between his knees. With a long gliding movement he pulled the knife towards him, paring the leather on each side. Sometimes the knife would slip and he would nick the soft leather of the upper.

"God damn ye for a contrary shoe," and then to anyone watching, "Will ye go out to play like a good child and let me get on with the job; I'll put the sole on baw-wise if I'm not careful."

He never really meant us to go. He re-set the shoe on the

last for the final tackings and, proud of the job when it was done, he would hum quietly to himself as he heated the waxy blacking stick on the open flame of the gas-stove. This he ran around the sides of the shoe to cover up any blemishes or knife-nicks before leaving the shoes outside the door to dry.

By early evening all our preparations for Sunday were complete and a calmness settled over the house. The food was stocked up, the house smelled of Sunlight soap and Mansion polish; shoes were polished and placed in a line at the kitchen door and clean clothes were laid on bedroom chairs. My mother took a bowl of big green cooking apples and sat at the front-room window, peeling and chopping them for Sunday's apple-cake while she watched the world go by. We collected the butts of the apples, dipped them in the saucer of sugar, and went out for a last hour of play before bed.

# Sunday

"MAM?" THE SQUEAK in my voice was a dead give-away. My mother looked up from the Sunday paper spread out on the table. "I have to have my heel turned by tomorrow morning." I dragged my grubby knitting from my schoolbag.

"You know you can't knit on Sunday!" Madge turned from her scrapbook. She had just spent her Sunday penny in Granny Redmond's and was marshalling her cardboard cut-outs for swopping in school next day.

"No knitting or sewing on Sunday; that's what the catechism says," Babs chimed in.

"Which catechism? It says nothing about knitting or sewing in my catechism." I was belligerent, not sure which side my mother would favour. My father looked over his glasses. "Little birds in their nests agree..."

"Unnecessary servile work on Sunday is what the catechism means," my mother said, "and I think in this case the turning of the heel of your sock has become necessary." I handed the knitting to her gratefully, but she was not finished. "This," she said, "is the very last time that knitting or sewing for Monday morning, which you should have done on Friday when you came home from school, will be classed as necessary. Clear on that point?"

My mother and father were practical people who did not go overboard in the strict observance of the injunction that no physical work should be undertaken on Sunday. Even so, they regarded it as a day of rest. My mother would never wield a paintbrush or clip the hedge on Sunday, nor would she wash clothes or take down the iron to press them, and my father wouldn't dream of digging the garden or hammering a nail. No shopping was done either, and with the exception of the sweetshops and the dairies, all shops were closed in the solemnity of the day.

On Saturday nights I went through the agony of putting rags in my hair, and in bed I tossed and turned and kicked Babs as I tried to endure the stiff pointers which would give me a pretty head of curls to show to the world in the morning. My sisters' heads of hair curled at the sight of a comb, but mine was long and straight and refused to curl of its own free will. I did not want to be Shirley Temple; I was quite content to be Jane Withers, the plainer of the two Hollywood idols, and wear my hair in a straight fringe, but that did not satisfy my mother who wanted curls on Sunday and two tidy plaits for the rest of the week.

"You've a little farthin' face," she would declare as she wound the rags round my stubborn hair. "We have to try and make somethin' of you."

Sunday started with Mass. Although the pattern of our Mass-going changed as we got older, my father's routine remained constant: Sunday morning meant Mass in Meath Street or with the Augustinians in John's Lane, where he could meet up with his friends and visit his old haunts. Religion, my father led us to believe, was not of any great consequence to him.

"I've no time for the craw-thumpers," he said, resisting my mother's efforts to have him attend what he called a "fire and brimstone" preacher. "Religion is best left to the women, and there's enough of ye in it to pray that my soul will not be damned in hell." But he carried his rosary beads wherever he went, dropping them in his pocket matter of factly and without ostentation, and during the week he stole quietly from the house for early Mass. I was often awake as he tiptoed down the stairs and sometimes I sneaked into the kitchen while he was making a pot of tea – breakfast for him and a cup to take to my mother before he left.

"I declare to God, child, but you put the heart crossways in me. It's only gone half-six. What has ye up at this hour?"

"I was awake early."

"Like father, like daughter."

"Can I come with ye?"

"Your mother'd kill me. It's a long walk to John's Lane, and it's too early for you to be out. Go back to bed like a good girl." But one day my legs were longer and I was bigger and on an occasional summer morning I did join him on the long walk to John's Lane church, proud to be trotting beside his hurrying figure. It wasn't the Mass that attracted me so much as the knowledge that I was doing something different, walking through the city while the rest of the world was still asleep. Hurrying along the streets in the early morning was something that I was sure none of my friends were doing, and gave me a great feeling of freedom and independence. My father saw no reason to worry about my walking the long journey home on my own, so long as the morning was bright and I was back in time to be ready for school.

Before we made our Holy Communion we did not have to fast, and on Sunday my father could be persuaded to take two of us to church with him. Those Sunday mornings were hushed somehow. The factory-hooters and sirens which screeched out the half-hour and quarter-hour warnings on weekdays were silent, and even at eleven o'clock the little streets where we walked were deserted. Up by the canal the barges were tied up, and the bargemen looked unfamiliar in their Sunday clothes as they clambered up their hatchways. The big doors of the granary were closed. We turned right at the harbour and into a deserted world, freed from the hustle and bustle of the week, and our shoes rapped and tapped in the silence. The tracks which crossed and recrossed the streets around the brewery were empty, the toy-trains of Arthur Guinness safely locked behind big wooden doors until the early hours of Monday, when they would be filled with grain for the brewing vats and coal for the furnaces, and racket on their way.

These were the streets owned by Guinness's brewery. Breweries had been established in this part of Dublin in the thirteenth century; St James's Gate, which gave its name to the firm, had once been an entrance in the city's ancient walls. In the 1690s Sir Mark Rainsford had a brewhouse here making beer and fine ales; it passed to a Huguenot named Paul Espinasse and thence to Arthur Guinness in 1759. Arthur was the eldest son of Richard Guinness of Celbridge, who was agent for Dr Price, the bishop of Meath, and the story told in the Liberties was that father and son had learned their trade brewing table-beer for the bishop. By the late 1800s the firm which Arthur Guinness established had become an empire. Properties surrounding St James's Gate were acquired and the streets of the brewery were born. Here a great labour force was formed – manual and white-collar workers, craftworkers and chemists, all for the brewing of beer from hops and barley, and a drink which Henry Grattan once called "the natural nurse of the people".

We walked down Marrowbone Lane, a wide uninteresting street with tenements on one side and high grey walls of factories on the other. At the junction with Summer Street it narrowed and the character of the street altered. It became a little village. There were small houses along one side and a long garden which led to what we always referred to as the Widows' Home, though whether widows actually lived there or not I never found out. On the other side was a solid public-house, and a row of tiny huxter shops huddling together until they lurched around the corner and became the start of the circle that was Thomas Court Bawn.

"A bawn is supposed to be a garden," my father explained patiently. "We had bawnogues in front of every cottage when I was a little lad in Wicklow. Your grandmother, if she was alive today," he said musingly, "would tell ye that she had cabbages and scallions in her bawnogue, and there was always the fuchsia bush and the dog-roses."

Thomas Court Bawn was no ordinary place to me. I always thought of it as my special courtyard. It was filled with the sounds of cocks crowing and geese cackling, the jingling of milk cans from the dairies and the clap-clapping of horses' hooves on the uneven cobbles. This was an oasis of country life dropped into a teeming city.

Inside the narrow opening to the bawn stood a dairy and houses with tiny gardens. Set in the wall was the Memorial door, or the fountain of the old Courthouse of St Thomas, the manor court of the Earl of Meath when he had established his seat here. There was an air of privilege about the Bawn, as there must have been when it was the courtyard of the manor, and somehow it had retained its ancient grandeur down the centuries, even though small children played in the dusty channels and in summertime the smell of sour milk and musty vegetables hung over everything.

All set in the curve of the bawn, some more shops, a dairy and a cottage gave way at the junction with School Street to the home of my mother's cousin, Granny Jordan. Granny Jordan had lifted her Wicklow roots and buried them deep in the soil of the Earl of Meath's Liberty. Her large house had outhouses extending up School Street, and in them she reared hens, geese and pigs and grazed a pony in her back garden. When my mother took me to Granny Jordan's to collect fresh eggs, the scent of the hay piled high in the loft and the warmth of her farmhouse kitchen always filled me with a longing for the country.

The Bawn held a tightly knit community with strong bonds of loyalty and neighbourliness. When night was drawing in, the darkness of the little court was slowly brightened by the lamplighter as he wound his way slowly from lamp to lamp. "Billy with the lamp, Billy with the light, Billy with the sweetheart out all night" was a rhyme which often followed him. The gaslight shed a golden glow on the butter standing on the counters of the little shops, and picked out the loose tea in wooden chests lined with silver paper, and the coal and turf and paraffin-oil hunched shoulder to shoulder on wooden shelves, while the corners of the courtyard outside filled with shadow and Thomas Court Bawn settled down for the night.

On Sunday morning we could not linger there too long because the bells were quickly ringing, calling us to church. My father could distinguish the different peals and tell whether we were late or early. Dolphin's Barn chapel we could hear from far behind us; Donore Avenue was a small clear sound, as it should be because it was only a chapel-of-ease; but as we neared the end of the Bawn we could hear the older, rounder bells of Saint Catherine's, the Meath Street chapel.

"Them bells are Becket's bells." My father held our hands tightly as we hurried on.

"Do you mean Becker's bells?" I didn't know that Becker,

the tea merchants in George's Street, where my mother bought our tea, owned any bells and I reminded myself to have a good look the next time I was there.

"No, I mean Becket's bells. Some day you'll learn all about it in your history books. Years and years ago this place belonged to a monastery of monks. They were told to build a church in honour of a holy man named Becket who was murdered in England. And they say," he went on, "that that's why there's such a *rí-rá* of bells and such a clatter of chapels and convents; to make up for the terrible deed that was done." And then the convent bells rang out – the Mercy, the Charity, the Presentation and the Holy Faith – and I took in what my father had said and Thomas Court Bawn became even more special. My highly tuned imagination brought all the ghosts of the place to walk with me. I met the monks in their well ordered orchards, their heads bowed in prayer, and I nursed their secrets to myself.

"The bells of John's Lane," he pointed to them as we got nearer our destination. "See that tower there? They swing off of ropes to keep the bells going."

"But our bell is pulled from the outside," I said, thinking of the altar-boys who swung out of the bell-rope at Donore Avenue. I resented the fact that pulling the bell-rope was a boy's job and no girl got a chance to do it.

"But there's more than one bell up there," my father said, as proudly as if he owned them personally, "and they're the best bells in Dublin."

"Even better than Christchurch?" I asked.

"Much better than Christchurch, and in any case Christchurch doesn't ring all Sunday morning and during the week. They have only one Service on Sunday."

"Don't they have Masses like we do?"

"No. They're Protestants and Protestants don't have Mass.

Hurry up now and stop chattering. We don't want to be late."

As we got nearer the church we joined a river of people, walking, hurrying, shuffling along streets which were free of the traffic of horses today. They streamed along, calling to one another, criss-crossing one another's paths, boys in their short-trousered suits and girls in Sunday hats; men with stiff-necked suits and ladies in crinkling taffeta skirts, holding them up carefully with one hand. We stood beside my father as he stopped to chat to friends outside the chapel door. They patted our heads and pressed pennies into our hands. We held back, saying shyly, "We're not allowed to..."

"Who's to know?" they said. "Sure, the fairies put it there."

Then it seemed as if the doors of the chapel had burst open as the sound of the organ swelled and the voices of the congregation rose in the opening hymn of the Mass. We went in to a fairyland of candles gleaming like golden stars against the polished wood, and the sun throwing colours of green, red and gold through the stained-glass windows above the altar.

If the rain did not spill out of the heavens, we walked back down Meath Street and, picking our delicate steps over the brus and leavings of Saturday night shoppers and dealers, we came to the little curving lane where the bird market was. We never bought a bird, but we loved to stop and look. We crossed the road to the park, where my father could let us loose. We raced around the paths and climbed over seats, causing the old men who had been pottering along at their ease to jab their sticks in the ground in annoyance and shout at us to behave ourselves.

St Patrick's Cathedral stood at the side of the park. Sister de Paul had explained to us in school that a cathedral was much more important than a church, and I was itching to see inside either of Dublin's two cathedrals, though neither of them were Catholic.

"Can I go in, just to see?" I asked my father.

"No, you can't. Catholics are not allowed inside Protestant churches."

"Would it be a mortal sin if we did?"

"I don't know, and we're not going to find out."

The following morning in school I broached the matter with Joan.

"I'll tell you what," I said.

"What?"

"I don't know if you'd be on for it..."

"On for what?" Joan said impatiently.

"On to see the inside of a Protestant church."

Joan's face paled. "We'd be excommunicated!"

"We could let on that we pushed the door open by mistake on our way home."

"I'll let on to nobody for you or anybody else!" Joan squealed.

So the mystery of what went on in Patrick's remained unsolved. To us, Protestants seemed very different. They lugged huge prayer books around with them and looked very posh and nose-in-the-airish – but my father insisted they were not. They were just the same as the rest of us, he said: God made us all.

When I made my First Holy Communion I forfeited the right to accompany my father to Mass. A command from somewhere on high insisted that we attend the children's Mass in Donore Avenue. I resented it. I was an early riser and could have gone to an earlier Mass.

"What ails you?" my mother asked as I dragged my feet around the kitchen. "You're in and out of here like a fiddler's elbow."

"Sunday mornings are too long and I'm hungry."

"You can stay hungry then; if you stayed in bed like the rest of them, you wouldn't be tempted. Keep away from that bread-crock!"

The devil was tempting me to break the fast.

"I'm going to get weak this morning," I confided to Betty one Sunday as we pulled on our grey-and-red knitted suits. I was proud of our knitted suits. My mother had spent hours devising patterns and knitting them from Killowen four-ply wool. One was a lovely soft grey, edged in red on the neck, sleeves and ribs; another was a more startling pattern of yellow and brown stripes, which we called our tiger suits.

"I'm sure I'll get weak this morning," I repeated as I struggled with the chemise top.

"Don't be a gom," Betty snapped; "we don't get weak."

But some children did get weak from the long fast. They slumped over during Mass and were fussed over and put sitting on wobbly chairs and looked beautiful as a glass of water was held to their pale dry lips.

The ten o'clock children's Mass was supervised by the nuns from Weaver's Square and the Christian Brothers from Saint Teresa's Preparatory School. Monday was sometimes a day of reckoning in school if you had spoken during the Mass, not genuflected or joined your hands when you should, spent too much time sitting and not enough kneeling, or poked your neighbour to make more room on the seat.

We always aimed to be in church before the nuns and to take our seats up at the top. The long rigmarole at the beginning of the Mass was very boring and my prayer-book certainly seemed much shorter than the priest's; I guessed that because his was in Latin it took him longer to get his tongue around the words. I liked to hear the gong sounded by the head altar-boy. It meant we had come to the parts I could understand.

"Kneel down when you hear the Sanctus bell – that's the

three bells sounded together," Sister Angelus told us. "You only remain seated if you're sick or have a sore knee." Scabby knees were a problem; one knee or other was regularly in the ward, so we ended up kneeling sideways or with one leg stretched out behind us.

"Join your hands and watch the altar until you hear the single warning gong." This meant the Consecration was about to take place. The bell sent everybody to their knees, old men spreading handkerchiefs to save their Sunday trousers from the dusty wooden kneelers.

"Bong," went the gong again and we lifted our heads. Up to this we could not see what the priest was doing on the altar because he had his back to us, but now he turned and raised the huge white host above his head. "My Lord and My God," we silently intoned.

I loved this magic part. Sister Angelus said that in this one moment God came down on the altar to us. The enormous silence, the lifting of everybody's head at the same time, the six large candles like giant sentinels, the gold braid on the priest's vestments and God made man in that big white host... I held the moment in wonder for as long as I could. Then the magic silence was broken as people began to cough and blow their noses loudly, and a great rustle of noise passed over the chapel.

Staying for another fifteen minutes after Holy Communion became a penance because I could almost smell the fried bread my father would have waiting for us when we got home. Sunday breakfast was a major part of the day. My father cooked, standing in the kitchen in his shirt-sleeves with his collar hanging from its button. He took the cast-iron pan and heated it on the gas flame until it spat at him, then sprinkled it liberally with salt and scrubbed it with paper until it was ready for frying. For himself and my mother there were rashers, sausages and black-and-white pudding, and we had crisply fried bread in beef dripping, fried tomatoes, white pudding and a little gypo, which we soaked up with bread.

"Rashers and sausages are too rich for young blood," my mother said.

"Too greasy for young skins," my father agreed, sneaking pieces from his plate on to ours, as my mother pretended not to see.

Sunday was dressing-up day for my father. "Have the collars come back from the laundry?" he would ask as he prepared himself for shaving. Collars were taken to the laundry to be stiffened, and when they returned shiny and hard we were not allowed to touch them. We brought them wrapped in cellophane paper to my father as he shaved before the mirror in the kitchen, patching his face with bits of newspaper whenever he nicked himself. He struggled with the unyielding collar, pressing the studs into the starched button-holes which joined collar and shirt together, stretching his neck up and back to ease the discomfort and swearing under his breath. He jutted his head and stretched his arms and then reached for the suit which he had taken from the big mirror-fronted wardrobe. He brushed it until every last speck of dust disappeared; we took turns to hold it for him while he lowered himself into the jacket and adjusted the red silk handkerchief and matching tie.

My father cleaned and pressed his own suit. "Go to the chemist," he instructed me one day, "and get me a couple of pennorth of salts of ammonia. There's one or two stains on the jacket and the seat of the trousers is getting shiny." I ran to the chemist and carefully lifted the folded packet he gave me and turned to run back, but curiosity got the better of me. I stopped and sniffed the packet in my hands. All at once my nose joined forces with my forehead and my head nearly

lifted from my shoulders. Fear lent wings to my feet and I
dashed in the kitchen door, screaming that I was poisoned. I
received little sympathy – a smack on my bottom and a long
lecture on curiosity.

"DON'T LOLL AROUND outside; if you can't find something to
do, come inside and I'll give you plenty."

Dressed in our Sunday best there was little we could do except sit on somebody's railing and admire each other's finery.
We could play skipping in a genteel sort of way, but we had
to be wary not to tear our fragile dresses or pull threads from
our knitted suits. Sometimes, if somebody had a bicycle, we
could bribe them with our Sunday pennies and line up to
have a scorch, but mostly we just sat around and talked.

We were discussing the altar-boys who, as we saw it, had the
best deal as far as the Church and indeed the rest of the world
was concerned. None of us girls would ever become altar-
boys.

"It's just not fair," Ann said angrily. "Why do boys have all
the best things to do?"

"Because they're boys. You heard what Sister de Paul said
last week."

"Why can't girls be priests?" The question had been fired at
her from the back of the class. No one owned up to having
asked it: you didn't put questions like that; it was nearly as
cheeky as asking "Where do babies come from?" Sister de
Paul had run a finger around the inside of her wimple, flung
her three-quarter veil over her shoulder and answered stoutly:
"Because women are not allowed into the sanctuary of the
church."

"What's the sanctuary of the church?"

"Beyond the altar rails; no girl or woman can go beyond the
altar rails – and that's enough questions for this morning."

"Little sissies, with their red buttoned dresses and lace on their surplices." If we couldn't join them, we could abuse them.

"I've got a threepenny piece; let's go and buy chocolate." Joan was tired of the altar-boys.

"Thruppence is a lot to spend on chocolate," Ann said, a little shocked. "Ye could get a whole Half-time Jimmy for that." Half-time Jimmy was a chocolate bar that was only bought at Christmas or Easter. "Where'd you get the thruppence?" she said, suspicious.

"The Aunt Bridie was up Saturday. She just got her summer diddly and she was handin' out money like snuff at a wake."

"Let's go; we'll go round the front way."

"No," I said. "You know we're not supposed to go that way on a Sunday."

"Who's to know? Let's chance it."

We all knew why we were not to go that way. The men of the pitch-and-toss school gathered on an open space where the Back of the Pipes met with Emerald Square. On Sunday mornings after last Mass they were there, huddled against Mr Adie's gable wall in sunshine or in rain, ready to gamble away the afternoon and more. How far they travelled to reach the game, and who spread the word that one was on, was always a mystery. They came silently from around corners and out of doorways, or a man might glance nonchalantly over his garden wall and then slip quickly out the back gate. Furtive figures, they moved singly, until they came together and formed a ring of shuffling figures stamping their feet, rubbing their hands and hunching their shoulders into the starched collars of their Sunday shirts, almost as if they were enacting a ritual dance.

"There won't be two ha'pence left to jingle on a tombstone for some of them," we had overhead our mothers say.

"There'll be some who were rollin' in it when they went there, and they'll go home skint."

"And some poor mother will be up to her ears in debt come next Friday. Ye'd hardly credit how much they spend."

Drawn by a mixture of curiosity and apprehension we sometimes ventured within seeing and hearing distance of the school.

"Care to earn a wing, son?" the gamblers would ask the boys. "We want somebody to keep nix in case the polis come." The pitch-and-toss school was positioned so that the men had three or four means of escape should the police get wind of a gambling session in progress. The sight of a police-car or a lone bobby on a bicycle was enough to send us all racing for the safety of our garden gates in case there was a rucky-up.

From outside the magic circle we could see little. The coin was tossed high in the air, the circle widening as heads shot up to follow its arc and tightening again as the men surged forward to see where the penny lay. Shouts of "The wing's a harp" meant nothing to us, but the sight of a man with a leather strap swishing at the gamblers' legs to keep them back, and the silent concentration of the men, gave us a shivery feeling.

To cure our boredom on Sunday my mother always planned something for the afternoon. We trudged miles to pick black-berries on the Crumlin Road, miles into town in winter to see the shop windows, miles in summer to the People's Gardens in the Phoenix Park. May meant walking miles to the procession in the new Lourdes Grotto in Inchicore.

"You've a face on you like a wet weekend; hurry up and get ready."

"Do we really have to go?"

"Yes you do, and I've just seen Jennie and her mother and the rest of the family go past."

I perked up. "Are they wearin' veils?"

"Yes, and so are you." I could argue and sulk the whole way to the procession, but it would be no use.

We walked up by the canal where it separated our walkway from the big grey wall of the Union, over which the tiny windows of the hospital building followed us like so many eyes. The South Dublin Union was in the care of the Sisters of Mercy, and besides the buildings for the poor and destitute it now held the only TB hospital in the city, the Rialto Hospital. "Consumption has no pity for blue eyes and golden hair," was a line I often heard recited, and I was glad that mine were brown. The Rialto gate, which we passed on our way, was always locked and guarded and entry was by pass only.

We walked past the row of cottages at St James's Walk. At the junction with Rialto Cottages stood a concrete tower which housed a bell, my father said, pointing. "Years ago it called the Guinness labourers to work."

The procession done, we had a glorious freedom on the way home. We came by the canal bank, a rough path with little hills and hollows, and small rivers to jump if it had been raining. When we came this way in autumn we could pick the blackberries which abounded on this long stretch of waterway.

The canal barges, though, were the biggest attraction of all, and we would happily spend hours just watching them passing by, the bargemen steering their bulky crafts expertly with the long iron arm of the rudder, which seemed to come out of the floor of the boat. The Grand Canal took the boats from the city, past Ranelagh, Portobello and Dolphin's Barn. At Suir Road bridge it was joined by a branch coming from James's Street harbour, used by the Guinness brewery for transport of their product to the flat lands of Kildare and

thence to the Shannon. Just above where the two canals con-
verged were lock-gates and beside them a tiny cottage where
the lock-keeper, his wife and family lived. How we envied
them. Those children could watch the barges as often as they
liked.

The sighting of a barge was the signal to take a rest. We sat
on the grass near the lock-keeper's garden, well away from the
stone slabs which bordered the lock-gates and which could
become slippery with splashing water. The barges shunted
into the stone-walled basin of the lock while the upper water
was held back behind the huge wooden gates. When the
barge came to the lock-gates, the water from the upper
stretches was released, and from our perch we watched it gush
forward and the barge rise slowly out of the trough. The
sweating lock-keeper worked the opening mechanism until
the lock-gates were parallel with the canal banks, swearing at
any venturesome boys who, as the barge drew level, jumped
on to the deck of the boat, chased along its length and
hopped clean on to the opposite bank. When the lock-gates
were being closed all of us helped to push the long handles
back until they straightened and formed a little footbridge
across the foaming water. We waited for the level of the water
to subside and then skipped over and back along the wooden
walkway, as sure-footed as any mountain goat.

The Guinness barges had their own quay at the little harbour above Echlin Street, where they crowded together like a
little village. There was always someone around them, the
bargemen in their blue and red gansies and men in overalls
fixing and mending. Mounds of coiled rope were loosed from
round granite pillars as the barges slid from mooring to
mooring, belching and burping as they were skilfully
manoeuvred up the short stretch. The Guinness harbour was
peaceful and placid as a lake, but dangerous in its depth, and

when we used this way on our journeys to the library in Thomas Street, we were warned to be very careful of our footing on the oily cobblestones and on the little iron bridge which spanned the water.

The comings and goings along the waterway were a part of our every day. During the war years when fuel was scarce, we watched the great big grey and brown shire horses working in relays to haul the barges along. These huge animals plodded slowly by, nodding and shaking and lifting their great shaggy hooves, ignoring us as they got on with the job in hand. What went on in their minds? I wondered. What did they think about as they stomped along, pulling their trailing ropes, like great adventurers heading for the land of God knows where.

Our house was so close to the canal that in the early morning we could hear the barges chug-chugging past. It was a comforting sound because it drowned the eerie screeching of the banshee which lived in the hollowed oak tree in old Mr Davis's house across road. The banshee was a tiny old woman no bigger than my sister's rag doll, and she came to warn people of death. To blot out the vision of the haggard banshee, with her long streaming hair and red-rimmed eyes, I would conjure in my mind's eye the long black snout of the canal barge forging a smooth passage, the water gently parting before it and bending the tall reeds at the canal's banks. When I heard that gentle chugging sound I would snuggle under the bedclothes and imagine the golden lights of the boat's lanterns and the bargeman, pipe in mouth, navy cap clamped on his head, and my world was safe from banshees for one more night.

By the time we reached home after our long day's journey, we were tired and quiet just as our mother wanted us to be. When my father divested himself of his starched collar and good suit and eased his feet from his shoes, we knew that Sunday was nearing its end. He settled himself in front of the brown wireless, and silence was observed in the house while he listened to the Foley Family's goings-on, then Joe Linnane's question-time. In holiday time we were allowed stay up for the Sunday play, but during school term we frantically did our sums, learned the rivers of the world, and rhymed off multiplication tables, all of which had been forgotten about on Friday. My mother sorted clothes to steep for Monday's wash. Sunday was done.

# Spring Cleaning

"THE PAINTERS HAVE started on the lower roads," my father said one evening when he came in from work. He might just as well have dropped a bombshell.

My mother suspended her tea-pouring. "Oh, no," she said. "They're not going to change my hall-door."

"It looks as if you'll have no choice," my father said, spooning sugar into his tea.

"But we've only just got that lovely stain on; it was only done six months ago."

My mother was an individualist in a quiet, uncomplicated way. She did not like being part of the herd, as she saw it. We rented our house from Dublin Corporation at a fair rent, and she felt entitled to have a fair say in making it into a proper home. She could see no rhyme or reason for painting all the houses in our small estate the same dull green or red, or alternating the colours in a monotonous pattern.

"Box houses from a children's reader; that's what they look like," she said disdainfully. In the past her answer had been to wait for about a month after the painters had finished and then set off to Stiles in Meath Street to select her own choice of colour for the door. She was skilled with a paintbrush. My father did the rubbing-down of the paintwork and she applied the brush.

This time it was different. Six months previously she had saved and hoarded and hired a local man to do a really good job of "graining" the hall-door. This was a specialised job of applying varnish to the wood and then using combs and cloths to produce a mock effect of wood-graining. The finished work, gleaming with coats of varnish, was her pride and joy.

"I'll go to the rent office in the morning," she said, "and see what I can do."

My father did not hold out much hope. He knew she was up against authority and that nobody would be willing to allow her break the rules; and as he anticipated, the official at the rent-office declined to help her. Meanwhile the painters were advancing from house to house, drawing nearer and nearer her precious door.

My mother never asked favours of anybody, and she scorned the suggestion of appealing to the local Councillor.

"I'll go to the Housing Department," she told my father, and she did. She walked to Castle Street and sat in their offices for over an hour, but nobody was willing to make a decision.

"They said there was nothing they could do about it," she reported that evening. "They said it was out of their hands. They said they would contact the foreman on the job and that it was up to him."

"And what did you say to them?"

She took her time in answering, and then said quietly, "I told them that no painter would touch my varnished door so long as I was here."

This was so unlike our mother that we waited each day to see how the battle would develop. Two days later the foreman arrived. My mother, who had been keeping a vigil at the front window, saw him coming, and had the door open before he knocked.

"That's a nice job of grainin' ye have there, Missus," he said. My mother said nothing. "How long since it was done, Ma'am?"

"Six months."

A man carrying a battered tin kettle joined the foreman on the little narrow garden path. We stood in a bunch behind our mother.

"Good job, Jem, what d'ye think?"

The second man ran his eyes over the door. "Fine bit of grainin'. A pity to spoil it, Jack." They ran their hands over the polished surface and inspected the front windows which had been painted cream. "Good man at his job, Ma'am, whoever he was."

The foreman looked directly at my mother. "It'd be a waste of good money to strip that, Ma'am. I think we'll leave it. We'll save on the paint anyway." My mother, still angry at having been pushed from pillar to post, felt that the foreman could have taken her out of her misery earlier. The foreman felt he was being generous. There was a long, awkward pause.

"I wonder would ye mind boilin' up the old kettle to make a pot of tea?" the foreman asked. It was the olive branch.

She took the kettle. "Put that on the gas," she said to Madge.

"I'll come back for it in about ten minutes," the second man said, and the two of them turned to go.

"You're welcome," my mother said, and then to the foreman as he walked out the gate: "I'm grateful to ye for saving the door."

"You're welcome, too, Ma'am," he said. "I like good work when I see it."

The painters were a change from hopping balls and rolling marbles, and we spent hours marking their progress along the street. My mother worried about the blow-lamps which they used and warned us constantly to stay out of their reach. She need not have worried. The men would swear at us in no un-certain terms if we came within shouting distance of their tools, and it was necessary to shout; the noise generated by the little paraffin-powered contraption discouraged all normal conversation. When the wick was lighted, it hissed and splut-tered and eventually droned in a loud, menacing tone as the pale pinky-blue flame licked the paint off the woodwork. So intense was the flame that you could actually see through it, and somehow it reminded me of the Devil, with colourless pink-tipped flames shooting from his mouth. We admired the painters' skill, working a palette knife in their right hand in tandem with the powerful blow-lamp in their left, uncurling broad swathes of old paint from the doors and window-frames of our street.

I liked spring. There was extra time to play in the evenings and the prospect of soon getting out of heavy coats, hats, long stockings and wellington boots. I did not like the single-mindedness of my mother, who viewed spring as a time for cleaning the house from top to bottom. Preparations must be made for the great spring festival of Easter. Curtains and covers had to be changed, and steps taken to root out all the cobwebs which had secreted themselves in nooks and cran-nies, and now faced the searching light of day under my mother's yearly onslaught.

The spring cleaning started on the Monday of Holy Week. We would arrive home from school to find the front windows bare, with a film of window-white liberally spread to screen the inside of the room from inquisitive passers-by. The heavy brocade curtains which had gone up in the week before

Christmas were hanging over the backs of the chairs in the kitchen.

"When you've finished your dinner, I need a hand with the curtains." I began to hate spring cleaning with quiet intensity and slowed my eating, but it still had to be faced.

"Take two corners, one of you, and the other one take the other corners;" and with my mother ahead of us, we carried the curtains like a bier to the backyard. Holding on tightly, we whisked and whooshed the curtains, turning them over like a giant mat until every last bit of winter's dust had settled on us instead, covering our hair, swirling up our noses and into our eyes. We folded the curtains ready for packing away and then took out the heavy white Nottingham lace curtains from their moth-balled cardboard boxes and reversed the ritual. It was a tiring job for young arms.

Cleaning the parlour was a job that was not entrusted to us children. In there were my mother's most precious things: white china dogs, with floppy ears and imploring eyes, sat on the mantel-shelf below the bevelled mirror hanging on its chains. Pride of place was given to the ebony chiffonier with the red glass non-pareil, and nobody but my father or mother was allowed wash the precious, colourful basin-shaped glass ornament, with its elegant stem, and its delicate glass beads which tinkled in any draught of air. There were dark blue venetian glass cup-and-saucer sets, elegant teapots and the beloved china tea-set which proclaimed in gilt that love was the giver. My mother had bought it piece by piece over many weeks, until the whole set sat resplendent on the sideboard which faced across from the other wall to the chiffonier. Four spoon-backed upholstered chairs, the seats of which were fitted with loose covers every time the heavy brocade curtains were changed, stood at the walls, and two easy chairs and a sofa similarly dressed completed the furniture. Pink and white china figures of a boy and girl stood sentinel on either side of the mahogany-cased Westminster clock, whose sacred workings only my father touched. He set it ten minutes fast to trap us into perfect timekeeping, but failed. We had other ways of marking the hour.

"The clock's just chimed the quarter."

"That's daft. I didn't hear the horn yet."

"Is the chapel bell gone?"

"Ye won't hear it this morning; there's a fog down."

Proper time-keeping was of prime importance to my father, but my mother took time in her stride. "Don't worry," she would say, "that's your father's old clock again."

It was spring when we got the washing machine. Until then, every stitch of clothes was washed by hand in the kitchen sink. On Sunday evening my mother steeped the badly soiled clothes in the galvanised bath, and on Monday morning before we left for school we stepped over little piles of clothes sorted on the kitchen floor while my mother prepared for the wash, wiping the galvanised clothes-line free of rust and checking her supply of wooden clothes pegs. She could not bring herself to waste money on the luxury of having her clothes washed in the laundry.

"While I'm in the whole of my health, I'll do them."

"The whole of your health won't stop you from killing yourself if you work too hard," was my father's retort.

The laundry cart from the White Heather or the Swan laundries called on Monday morning, and those who intended to stay in the whole of their health handed out their miscellaneous washing in the large bags provided. The bags were returned in mid-week with the washing damp inside and only needing the flat iron heated on the gas to do the ironing.

But something unusual had happened this Monday morning. There was no hectic activity in the kitchen, no piles of clothes, no steam rising from pots on the black gas stove in the corner.

"What's wrong?"

"Nothing's wrong."

"Where's the washing?"

"There's no washing today. Your mother is taking the day off," my father said, looking as if he were bursting to tell a secret.

"Stop foostering about the lot of ye; you'll be late for school. And never mind your father," mother said, shooing us out the back door. "The washing will be done by the time you come home. Off with ye now."

But the washing wasn't done by the time we came home – my father was right in the middle of it, and enjoying himself immensely. Clouds of steam rose from pots hopping on the gas stove and the kitchen was swimming in water. He stood at the kitchen sink, his shirt-sleeves rolled up and his face streaming with perspiration, and beside him stood his new toy, a brand new washing machine.

"Look!" He pushed the handle to and fro and the wooden paddles low in the washing machine trundled the clothes backwards and forwards in the sudsy water. He lifted the lid so that we could see the wonders inside, while my mother hovered in the background, warning us to be careful not to tumble in. A hand-operated mangle stood beside the machine, and each piece of washing was offered up to the mangle. Father pushed the paddles of the washing machine while my mother operated the mangle. We all tried our hand at the mangle with my mother instructing us how to fold the clothes before we put them through.

"Don't put them in baw-wise; they'll come out crooked and creased; take your time." Casual mangling left the clothes so creased that no amount of hot ironing would smooth them.

Ferrying gallons of water from the stove to the machine, my father washed everything in sight that day. We ended up with the cleanest floorcloths we had ever had, and, at the peak of our enthusiasm, even the paint rags went for a wash.

"Who sees whether it's clean or not?" I said wearily as I held on to my mother's long skirt while she stretched out the bedroom window to wash the paintwork. She liked to have an assistant on hand when she tackled "high up" jobs in one of her spring cleaning sprees.

"I see it," she said, "and what's more, I expect you to see it too, and take the good example I'm setting you. I'm not doing this for the good of my health. Cleanliness is next to Godliness, remember."

"I don't know how God comes in to it," I muttered to myself as I clattered the chair she had been using down the stairs. "I sincerely hope and pray to God that there's no spring cleaning in heaven!"

# A Letter From the Country

"THERE'S A LETTER from Aunt Mary."

A letter from Aunt Mary could mean only one of two things: somebody had died that she thought my mother should know about, or some of us were being invited to stay with her for the summer holidays which were just about to begin.

"She'll be able to take three of you next week for a few weeks."

"Oh."

"Don't you want to go to the country?" My mother turned from her ironing at the kitchen table, took the black iron from the gas flame where it was heating, and tested it with the tip of a wet finger. It hissed and she put its fellow in its place on the cooker.

Every year when the school holidays came around I felt exactly the same way. The invitation always came and was always accepted, but the feeling of homesickness at the thought of leaving Dublin increased as I got older, leaving me cold and apprehensive. It clouded what I knew in my heart: that I loved the countryside and was always happy there. I could never quite crystalise the conflicting feelings and was left with a sense of unease. I even went so far as to hope that somehow the invitation would not materialise; that I had got too old for Aunt Mary to handle or that she had decided she didn't want any of us Dublin jackeens anymore.

"I don't know; I don't like the long bus journey and... I feel strange for the first few days. Can I give it a skip this year?"

"You know you love your Aunt Mary's." My father had come into the room. "Don't worry about the bus journey. We'll get you a seat near the top of the bus, and you can have sugar-barley sweets to suck on the way."

"What would you do here for the whole summer holidays? There'd be nothin' for ye to do," my mother said in a coaxing voice. This was the first time I had voiced my reluctance to visit my country relations, and she was not quite sure what to make of it. She was also thinking about how she would occupy us for the long six weeks holiday, because if I did not go, then neither would Betty and Tess. She looked at me as she ironed and folded the summer dresses she had been preparing since the letter arrived. I knew she was right. We were the envy of our schoolfriends because we had somewhere to go, somewhere away from the hot city streets, somewhere different to see.

Aunt Mary was my mother's widowed cousin, related to her on her mother's side of the family. Transplanted from the Liberty of St Thomas because of a family legacy to her husband, she had reared nine children, all now grown men and women, on a small mountainy farm close to my grandfather's old home in County Wicklow. She saw it as her duty to give my mother's small children the benefit of a country rearing for some weeks of the year, the benefits she could not see in the streets she had left behind – clean fresh air, plenty of farm-fresh food, and above all the freedom of the countryside.

Stepping on to the bus at Burgh Quay for the fifty-mile journey upset me, but I never could find the courage to jump out and tell my father that I had changed my mind. I sensed that had I done so he would not have known what to do, nor would the driver in whose care he had placed us.

As the Carlow bus drew into Hacketstown, the sugar-barley sweets long since disappeared, my Dublin streets seemed millions of miles away. The bus turned and belched its way out the Carnew road, leaving us sitting on our cases outside the hotel, dismally aware that all connection with home was broken.

"D'ye think they'll have remembered to meet the bus?" Betty and Tess were near to tears. It was my responsibility now to be the older sister.

"Of course they'll remember."

A donkey tied to a post near by brayed loudly, baring his enormous teeth and gums and rolling his eyes at us. Hens squabbled in the confines of a cart. As we sat by the side of the street, men slouched past in thick hob-nailed boots, women in long skirts and strong farm-boots turning to look at us. Children stared with open curiosity, until we dropped our eyes, feeling confused and alone in an alien world. We need not have worried. A pony and cart arrived at the top of the town with cousin John sitting inside, trying to hold the pony back.

"Young 'uns," he shouted as he whoahed the pony to a standstill, "did ye think we'd forgot?" If we had, it did not matter now that he was here. He helped us scramble into the back of the dray and we sat on the dusty hay, staring back at the surprised faces of the local children who, caught out by this turn of events, turned and ran off.

The drive to the farmhouse was even bumpier than the bus. We bounced over stones and potholes, and the sudden jerking at the pony when John stopped to chat to somebody on the road had us falling forwards and sideways.

"Hould on to yourselves, girls, it's only Mick," and Mick –
or Pat or John-Joe or Sonny – wiped their hands quickly on
their trousers and stretched them out in greeting.

As the dray rattled into the yard, scattering the hens in
undignified flight, Aunt Mary's head appeared over the half-
door. She was a neat, tidy woman with a soft bun of white
hair coiled high on her head. She walked with the upper part
of her body bent slightly forward – not humped, but grace-
fully bent over, like one of the white ducks which came wad-
dling into the farmyard each evening.

"Mary," my cousin shouted to his mother. Her four sons always addressed her by her Christian name, except when she
crossed them in some way and then they called her "Mother"
in exasperated tones. "Mary, they've brought the puddings."

"Hould your whisht, can't ye, and let the children down."

"I've checked, Mary. Didn't I, girls?" and we nodded slowly,
holding on to the bags which Mother had entrusted to our
care. My mother always sent a contribution to our holiday in
the form of a generous supply of groceries; she sent raisins
and currants and Becker's tea, sugar, sweets and biscuits, but
most importantly she sent back-rashers and sausages and
black-and-white puddings from Hafner's in George's Street.

"Take off your good hats and coats, children." Aunt Mary
bustled to the fire where the kettle was hanging from a hook
on the chimney. "Hang them above in the parlour and let me
look at ye. I hope you've brought stronger shoes than those.
And that dress; when you've had your tea, change out of it –
it'll do tomorrow for Sunday Mass."

We carried our cases into the parlour, dark and unused and
filled with ornaments and old pictures. Back in the kitchen,
we swung our legs up on to the settle bed and waited for our
tea of soda bread and yellow salty butter. We would spend
many days sitting on the settle bed and on the seats by the

hearth, but now not even the lovely warm smell of the turf could banish a sudden longing for home, where the floor was not flagged and the walls were not whitewashed and giant shadows did not jump from the uncertain light of the oil-lamp placed in the deep shelf of the kitchen window. Home was where everything was clean and bright and at night-time light shone at the touch of a switch; here we carried a candle into the dim recesses of the bedroom.

In Aunt Mary's house the half-door stood open from early morning until late in the evening. During the day it provided light from outside, because the kitchen window was too small to be of any great use in brightening the room. The head and shoulders of a bulky neighbour framed in the half-door with his greeting of "God bless all here" could block out all light to the kitchen. At night the sounds of footsteps and bicycles carried from the road as we stood at the half-door, watching the clear night-sky with its myriad stars and the moon rising over Kyle Hill.

It was early to bed on that first night, and we cried a little and watched the Sacred Heart oil-lamp burning over by the corner. "See if there's a chamber-pot under the bed," Betty whispered to me. "You know you can't use the commode." And there was one placed there specially for us children at night. In the daytime we were expected to use the fields and the haggard; commodes did not come at two a penny, and not every house boasted one. They were certainly not bought with children in mind, but used exclusively by elderly visitors and people who were ill. There were no toilets or sinks in any farmhouse, and though an earthenware jug and basin was left in the bedroom for important visitors, washing was usually done with a dish of water on the kitchen table. More often than not, we children were given a piece of Sunlight soap and a towel and sent to the spout in the corner of the yard, where the ice-cold water flowed through a length of piping which came through a hole in the ditch.

I lay awake for a long time. The ticking from the big clock in the kitchen I could identify, but there was another, more faint ticking sound, and I thought of the death-watch beetle which was supposed to foretell a death in the family. I hid my head under the bedclothes for fear it was about to announce my death. I tried to convince myself that if I did not hear it, then I could not die, but still I tossed and turned in the bed, wishing that Aunt Mary in the upper room would not snore so loudly. Eventually, uncertainty drove me to creep from under the bedclothes and open the door between the two rooms. The sinister sound got louder and louder, and then I saw the bright green hands of Aunt Mary's alarm clock winking at me as it ticked merrily away.

We slept in the big lumpy bed in the lower bedroom which was next to the cowhouse, and through the slanted slot in the deep stone wall we could hear the cattle breathing. Next morning the sound of their lowing and the crowing of the cock on the dung-heap in the yard wakened us early.

It was a Sunday morning and we dressed in our best to go to Knockannana chapel. Waiting for us in the pony and trap, Aunt Mary was the picture of Queen Victoria, dressed in a stiff black taffeta dress with a jet-beaded coat and a black hat sitting neatly on her snow-white hair. John sat opposite her, balancing the trap so that the shafts lay easily on the pony's sides. We climbed up and the pony and trap set off, but as always we only got a mile out the road.

"Stop the trap, John," Aunt Mary ordered, and then to the three of us: "Step down now like good children; your legs are young and we'll give Mrs Hayes a lift." John would wink at us, but I fumed inside at Mrs Hayes for not having a trap of her own.

As we walked along the dusty road, we drew the attention of curious eyes: we were strangers. But tomorrow we would be less so, because on our first Monday we did "the visitations", as we liked to call them. Visiting the neighbours' houses was a custom that had to be observed. As the years went on, I began to question why we were slaves to custom, but still we went, calling to every house near by. The nearer houses we were sent to visit on our own and this was a terrifying experience. One, two, sometimes three dogs ran out to challenge us, and we were no Cuchulainns as we picked stones and skeughs from the ditches.

"Don't run!" I instructed my sisters as we stood petrified at the yard gate. "Don't let them see you're frightened." They rushed at us from every corner of the farmyard, scattering ducks and hens in their path. We called to them or pitched stones at them, praying all the time for help to appear from the farmhouse. A head shouting from the half-door sent the dogs slinking away with their tails between their legs, but the more daring yapped and barked until they were kicked howling to the end of the yard.

"Come in, children, come in. My, but you've grown since last year. Sure I wouldn't know ye at all. Sit there beside the fire and let us have a look at ye. The dead spit of your mother."

"Now who's this you're like. D'ye think she's like the grandmother?"

"Oh no, she's the other side of the family entirely."

We sat beside the fire and drank buttermilk or sweet milk, while out of the corner of my eye I could see little children scuttling against the dresser. We enjoyed a nicely superior feeling; in our best dresses we were city-like, from a different world. But clothes were not so important and I knew the tables would be turned as we renewed our friendships with the neighbouring children. Theirs was an exciting life, of sitting on a three-legged stool while they soothed the jabbing hind-legs and swishing tail of the cows and drew milk in long fluid movements from their bulging udders. They taught us to bring the cattle home from the fields and helped us ride the pony to the forge to be shod. The first overtures were made when the adults had finished assessing us, and told the younger ones to "Walk your visitors a bit down the lane and see them on their way." Pushing and pulling one another, they darted off in secret short-cuts to tell the next farmhouse that we were coming.

The days became less strange and the nights more comforting as we settled into the rhythm of country life.

"The rosary, boys." Aunt Mary knelt beside a kitchen chair with her head in her hands, and sent us speeding to the bedroom to get our rosary beads which hung on the bedpost. Nobody dared move to *céilí* or rambling house until the rosary was said.

"You're right in time." A friend of John's had crossed the threshold.

"Mother of God tonight, Missus, I've just said the rosary at home."

"Well, nobody's leaving this house till we've said it," she said, "and it'll do your soul a power of good to say a second one, won't it?"

August Monday was the best time to be in the country. That was the weekend when it seemed every cousin we knew, and their fathers and mothers, came to Aunt Mary's. Because we had been there before them, we felt we had rights of residency, but we were shoved aside without ceremony to make room for the others. The house was full to bursting with people. It didn't matter where we slept. We children slept heads and tails in the big bed, and the old settle bed beside the open hearth could not count the heads it cradled. Mattresses were dragged out and placed on the cool cement of the dairy floor and even the parlour was pressed into service for the occasion.

All this for the harvesting of the oats. For days we would tramp the fields with our tall knowledgeable cousins and inspect the pearly-green crop, which was caressed and fondled and eventually pronounced ripe for reaping. I watched with a feeling of sadness as my cousin sliced the scythe through the trembling crop and the land was suddenly empty and bare. My father loved this August holiday trip and he took his place amongst the workers, bending and straightening, binding the sheaves and standing them in stooks to ripen in the sun, his face red with determination. Saving the oats was as important to him as it was to any farmer, and he kept watch on the stooks, turning them so that the heat of the lingering summer sun might turn the green harvest to light gold.

After the oats were cut my cousin would tap on our bedroom window at the first light of morning.

"I'm going to look for mushrooms; do you want to come?"

There was never a need to ask twice. I loved mushrooms, and as quickly as I could I dressed and slipped from the sleeping house. We searched the newly shorn fields for what the nuns had called the *fás aon oíche* – one night's growth. And like little balls of magic they would emerge as we walked among the prickly stubble, peeping from the wispy scarves of autumn mist which floated across the ground.

When we returned to the house, Aunt Mary had the black skillet-pot swinging on its hook beside the fire.

"Careful, child, careful," she would say as I lifted the lid to watch the belching bubbles break through the skin of the yellow-meal stirabout. I was told by Aunt Mary that the "yalla meal" was the salvation of the poor in the Great Famine of 1847, when grain ships from America brought the yellow maize or Indian meal after the potato had failed. In my heart I was sorry for the people who had lived though those awful years, but still I was glad that somebody had brought yellow meal to Ireland.

"Meal for the chickens, that's all it's fit for," I overheard a cranky old man mutter to himself as he passed by a sackful standing on the floor of a shop in Hacketstown, but I loved its slightly bitter taste and missed it when we returned to Dublin. With sweet milk or buttermilk, as the fancy took us, it made a morning and evening meal that none could better, and when we were finished we could squelch the layer of skin in the bottom of the skillet between our fingers and feed it to the hens.

With the breakfast cleared from the table it was time to do the day's baking. I leaned on the kitchen table and watched Aunt Mary as she set about it. I helped her bank up the turf until the heart of the fire glowed orange and red, then back to the table where she reached into the sack of flour and poured handfuls into a big bowl.

"Do you not have to measure the flour, Nanny?" I asked. We measured in school.

"Where d'ye think I'd get the time to do that, child?"

I had the can of buttermilk ready and she helped me pour it carefully into the well which she had made in the flour. That was as far as I was allowed go. Her strong hands mixed and swirled the paste with rapid movements until she had the springy dough just the way she wanted. Then the great mound was emptied on to the floured table and kneaded and pressed into a flat circle. Halfway through the kneading she stopped to swing the griddle pan on to the glowing fire so that it would be hot enough for baking.

"Can I have a piece of dough to make a cake?"

She pretended not to hear.

"Can I, Nanny?" She pulled the great circle of dough apart and shaped it into smaller circles, and then pushed a piece towards me.

I slipped down from the chair and borrowed a mug from the dresser. Punching and pulling my bit of dough, I used the mug to form half-moons and circles, and always I changed my mind halfway and had to pound the dough back into shape before starting again. Meanwhile Aunt Mary had slipped the first of her soda-breads into the round griddle pan, having dusted it generously with flour beforehand. I jumped down again to help. She put the flat lid on the pan and with the long tongs she took small glowing pieces of turf and placed them on the lid. This was the best oven I had ever seen. It was so simple, just the heat from the hearth and the red-hot embers on the lid.

Aunt Mary knew exactly how long it took to bake soda-bread and spent the best part of the morning filling the bottom shelf of the kitchen dresser with steaming hot loaves. My offering she placed on the centre of the hot lid, turning it with the tongs as she replaced the hot embers, but it was a sorry sight in the end and had to be fed to the chickens.

When the last fingers of daylight were streaking the darkening sky, the workers returned from the fields, weary, hungry and sunburnt. The house grew noisy and in the yard the men jostled one another to be first to the spout for a wash. The potatoes bubbled on the fire in the big skillet pot and the table was lined with knives and forks. A whole ham sat waiting with the big carving knife beside it, and we were sent running to the dairy for extra butter and milk, and told to keep out of the men's way. When everybody was finished eating, we helped to clear the table, while the men slouched out into the yard with their pipes hanging from their lips and a glass of porter in one hand.

"Go down to the parlour and get John's melodeon. It's time we made a start on the music. I'll get out the mouth-organs."

The women pushed the table back against the wall, where it could be used to seat half a dozen people. Hob-nailed boots began to scrape the kitchen flagstones and soon people were twirling in the steps of a half-set, the weariness of the day forgotten. We heard voices coming over the road as neighbours came rambling. The house seemed to fill with laughter and lilting voices until the night drew towards morning. Three of us pushed together in the seat by the fireplace and I could not remember falling asleep, but I woke as Aunt Mary was tucking us into the big bed. The kitchen was very close so I didn't feel left out, but I irritated Betty at the end of the bed by beating time to the music with my toes. It was impossible to sleep. I crept out and, slipping my cardigan about me, watched the departing figures, their bicycles clanking on the farmyard stone and the glow of somebody's pipe against the cowhouse wall.

Another week was left to us before we had to return to Dublin and school. We never strayed far from the farmhouse, because we had been told that "Sonny ate children", and there was also an eagle who lived on Eagle Hill beyond Hacketstown who carried little children away. I searched the sky every day for the eagle, but it never came; Sonny, however, was a figure who was very real indeed. He was a big man whose farm stretched across the valley from Aunt Mary's. He grazed sheep on the hill and his bulky form was regularly seen striding along our road. We were with John one day when he swung open the far gate to the hill and shooed some sheep in front of him.

"I've just been telling the young 'uns here that if you're hungry you sometimes eat chaps. Isn't that so, Sonny?" We backed away. Sonny swayed gently back and forth on his

the table when they were lifted from the scalding pot. And it was. Mugs of buttermilk and heaps of floury potatoes sat on the table, and the cooked rabbit was divided on to our plates.

Aunt Nanny's was a two-storey stone farmhouse. The bedroom floors creaked and groaned in the long summer nights, mysterious sounds to match the fitful shadows chasing across the moonlit walls. When the rustling of the dawn chorus nudged me awake, I crept to the window to look out. In the early morning mist, the gate to the orchard looked like the entrance to a magic world, and I watched for any tell-tale movement in the grass. My head told me I was too old to believe in fairies, but secretly I hoped for just one glimpse of a tiny dew-spangled creature.

I was brought down to earth in the brightness and practicality of the day. Aunty Nanny had a job for my cousin Mary and me.

"The red hen," she said, "will have to be watched. She's clocking." Convinced that the red hen was laying out, she told us to search the ditches and the orchard, but we found nothing. In the end we sat in the yard and waited. Our strategy worked. Suddenly we heard a triumphant cackling and we raced to the spot to find the eggs still warm and smooth.

And then the red hen was uneasy. She squatted on the dungheap at the corner of the haggard and scrabbled her yellow feet in the straw and the dust at the gate to the orchard. We followed her every day listening to her preoccupied cluck-cluck-clucking until eventually Aunt Nanny said: "Mary, get the basket and away with ye over the hill for setting eggs."

"Why do we have to get setting eggs?" I asked Mary as we set out that afternoon.

"Because we have no cockerel," she said, and she clamped her mouth shut at once, and I knew that I should not ask any further questions.

We bought a clutch of eggs, and fetching a box from the barn we filled it with straw, placed the eggs on top and brought it into the kitchen. With a sweep of her burnished wings the hen encircled the precious eggs, settling herself in the box with an air of great contentment. She dropped the grey hoods over her beady eyes, as if watching us from behind closed blinds, her tiny head snuggled in a ring of fluff around her neck. Muttering and cooing softly to herself, the red hen became part of the sounds of the kitchen, like the ticking of the grandfather clock. For three weeks she sat there, while I took turns in lifting her from the eggs every day, putting my hands gently under the warm bulk of her body, and feeding her until she nearly choked.

I was curled up on the floor at the window in the bedroom one morning when Mary shook me awake.

"Get up," she said; "the chickens are out."

I pulled the bedclothes off Tess and tumbled her out of bed. "The chickens," I shouted. "Mary says the chickens are out."

Below stairs there was a great fussing and fretting from the box by the hearth. I could not believe what I was seeing, as the tiny half-naked chicks poked through the shells and wobbled on spindly legs, their pink beaks open but uttering no sound.

One summer, Daisy, the mare, was in foal while we were there.

"She's going to have a baby," Mary explained as I jogged up the lane on Daisy's broad back. She helped me trace the shape of the foal in Daisy's swollen body, but its birth was guarded from our curious, inexperienced eyes.

"You can't – no, you mustn't go in there," Aunt Nanny said very firmly. "It's not work for women. It's work for the men. Here," she handed me a sack, "go to the field and get me some potatoes for the dinner."

Curiosity got the better of me and I sneaked up to the old stable door where Daisy was about to foal and peeped inside, but Uncle Dan saw me and shooed me away. I went off with the sack under my arm and found the drill of potatoes which was being worked. I took the fork and dug, shaking the soil from the shining potatoes, and I dragged my harvest back across the field.

"I'm going to be a farmer's wife," I confided to Tess on the way home to Dublin.

"How can you be a farmer's wife if you don't live in the country?" She shook her dark curls in disdain.

"I could always ask Aunt Nanny or Aunt Mary to let me live with them." Or maybe I'll marry a farmer, I thought, but I didn't say it.

"Oh, yes," my mother said when I put my plan to her. "And what will happen when the cold and the rain and the snow come in the front door every time you open it, and you have to wear wellington boots all day, and everywhere is cold and dark and mucky?" I hadn't thought of it like that.

Returning to Dublin was almost as hard as our first days in Wicklow had been weeks earlier. We had many things to boast about, but Mary and Joan and even Jennie soon tired of the telling, and they weren't really that interested. But I remembered the long golden days of summer, full of mauve foxgloves with yellow fairy-shoes, a hillside aglow with gorse and the woods full of purple-staining fraughan bushes; streams full of wriggling tadpoles and frog-spawn, and soft carpets of green where wild strawberries hid their flushed faces.

It would be another year before I could sneak crumbs from Aunt Mary's kitchen table to tempt the chickens on to the half-door, or sit in the well of the hearth and watch the sky through the open chimney, and wonder what my aunt had stored in the taileogue, the ledge which ran the width of the chimney-breast. Taileogue, crickeen, bawnogue, skeugh, scraw – I recited the words on the journey home and wondered who would whistle the men in from the bog with the long silver whistle which hung on the kitchen dresser. I could smell the soda-bread and the stewed tea which we carried in cans to the hayfield, past the hedges strewn with summer washing, over the stile and past the Mochain – the field of the big tax. I could see the hearth, where the fire must never be allowed go out, except when there was a death in the family, and I could hear the chat at night when we were safely tucked in bed and neighbours sat beside the fire, the lilt of their voices lulling us into drowsy sleep.

# Marble Red, Marble Blue

WHILE WE WERE in the country my mother used her time to prepare for the long winter which lay ahead. She made and mended our winter clothes, and when we came home she set up stockings on four needles, knitted the ribs, then handed us the rest so that we could learn to help.

As far as I was concerned, those black woollen stockings were a disaster. No matter how tight the rib, big black garters were always needed to keep them from falling down, and we lamented the time we spent pulling and straightening them. Also, thick hairy stockings were no match for rough concrete when we fell over in the schoolyard.

"You've a poppy in your stocking." The poppy would have grown bigger as we struggled home, the hand-knitted stitches loose and rambling. Cobbling was the only thing for it, and I reached for the rounded wooden cob in the darning bag hanging behind the kitchen door. I liked weaving the needle in and out and so I never minded darning, but the hole would be darned so often that soon there was a felted welt where the knee of the stocking should have been.

My mother believed in having us wear plenty of warm clothes. We wore hand-knitted woollen vests handed down from one to the next, and over these we wore stays or combinations. Then we had knitted skirts with calico chemise tops and the lot topped off with a long-sleeved jumper. Despite my father's warning that we had more peels on us than an onion, my mother knew that we needed the heavy warm clothing, not only in school, but also when we played outdoors in the evenings.

As the autumn evenings drew in we gathered on the street with our friends, free to spend our time playing all the games the season demanded. The messages were all collected after school, and homework left until dark. The hours between were ours for play.

Boys were disruptive and we made that very clear to them when we were about to organise any of our ball or rope games. Boys were butter-fingered when it came to hopping balls, or, even worse, when it was their turn to bounce the ball against a wall, they would cant it over somebody's garden fence and run off. So on the whole we left them severely alone. Girls ruled the roost, and we could neither be bullied, teased nor coaxed out of our position. We weren't above ridiculing them when they attempted to hop and skip and cross legs in time to exacting rhymes, which we were expert at. If they became bored with their own games, and we never thought any of their games very imaginative anyway, they could sometimes be cajoled into male roles, as doctors, ambulance men and, of course, fathers, when we played Mothers and Hospitals.

But at playing marbles, the boys were cocks of the walk.

"I'll trade ye, six marbles for your gullyer."

"No."

"Well, what about the taw?"

"What about it? I won them all; they're mine."

We bought marbles in Granny Redmond's shop beside the

Aughrim dairy on Marrowbone Lane. She sold marbles, scraps – cut-out figures of people and animals – pencils, sticks, sweets and lollipops. I was a little frightened of Granny Redmond, even though she had great value in marbles. She sat behind the counter and never seemed to leave it, day or night, and she wore what appeared to be a sack around her shoulders. I felt she always looked at us children with deep suspicion as she examined our pennies and halfpennies, turning them over and over in her hands, and counted out our marbles with knotted reddened fingers.

Glass or earthenware marbles were twelve or fifteen a penny and the glass marbles came in all colours of the rainbow, with ribbons of red, blue and green streaking through the solid lumps of glass. A gullyer was a large marble and a taw was a large earthenware marble. Leadeners could not be bought in the shops. They were ball-bearings, and a deadly weapon in the hands of a marble-player.

We played marbles on the kitchen floor until my mother got tired of kneeling figures that she could trip over or marbles that could take the legs from under her and she shooed us outside.

"Let's have a shootin' match." Ann's brother stood in front of her.

"Can't," she said. "I'm on me uppers."

"You've got a leadener; at least you had this mornin'. I'll put three glassiers to your leadener and I'll lend ye me taw to play."

We decided to take him on.

Joan and I added three marbles each to Ann's leadener, so there were nine glassiers in line, plus the leadener. Our marbles stood in a row at the top of the path.

"Toss ye for first go."

He won.

The first go had the advantage because he had the full shooting gallery ahead of him. We took up our positions at an angle to the marbles and the challenger walked from side to side and brushed pieces of paper or imaginary dust from the path of his killer. He lay on the ground and examined the angle of his drive.

"Will ye start for goodness sake. It'll be teatime before ye get a move on."

"I'll stop if ye like and go somewhere else. I thought you wanted to win some marbles."

"Do what you like," Ann said. "You called the game."

Suddenly her brother crouched on the footpath. He had a good eye and a steady hand, and in one swoop he wiped out half the line, including his sister's leadener.

The boys were more practised than us. As young ladies we could not play marbles all the way to school like they did; our dignity would have been sorely dented if we were caught playing in the muddy channel at the side of the road.

When we gathered to play in the evenings, the younger children were always in our care. We watched where they went and brought them into whatever game was being set up. Games were organised around them and they became children of the poor woman from Sandyland who had all her children by her hand and produced them one by one:

She can knit, and she can sew
She can make a lily-white bow
She can make a dress for the Queen
So please take one of my orphans.

We played ring-a-rosie for the younger ones and fell down, small and large bottoms all smacking the roadway. Jennie and I, Joan and Maddy were experts at bossing our younger sisters and brothers. We marched them up and down and made them sit, stand, turn and run whenever whichever game we were playing demanded. They shunted like trains to kill Jinny on the railway who was picking up stones, and they chopped with their chubby little hands all the robbers who had robbed my fair lady in Bow Lane. And we loved the wallflower song where they never turned their back on saucy Jack, but had to be twirled and twisted to do so.

As the evenings drew in, Betty and Tess were too young to be allowed out to play after tea, and Madge and Babs had reached the age when they had more responsible things to do than tear around the road and the playground. So it was usually Jennie and I, and such of our friends as we could muster, who played, "Red, rover, red rover, let Maddy come over," and held tight to each other as Maddy tried to find the weakest link to break through our chain of hands. If somebody had a Guinness rope we would chant:

Ever, Iver, chimney sweeper
Had a wife and could not keep her
Had another, did not love her
Up the chimney he did shove her

while the heavy coil of rope slapped lazily on the road and we jumped backwards and forwards until the rope was suddenly turned fully in an attempt to catch us out. The best fun was when a bunch of boys and girls all jumped in together and we skipped to

All in together, boys
This fine weather, boys
Nineteen, twenty
The rope should be empty

and we all scattered, laughing and pushing.

We did not want to hear the call of "You're wanted" when the lights came on in the houses and smoke rose from the chimneys against the darkening sky, telling us that night was closing in. "You're wanted," was the warning bell. Another game of Pussy-Four-Corners might be completed before the second message came.

"Mam says if you don't come this minute, you'll not be out to play for a week."

If we ignored that, my mother standing at the back gate looking steadily in our direction was enough to cause me to abandon rope, collect balls and walk demurely past her into the kitchen.

Coming into winter some of us always needed new shoes, and new shoes meant cardboard boxes. It had been my turn the previous Saturday and I was the proud possessor of my first grown-up shoes, with a bow on the front and a slightly raised heel. My interest in the shoes had waned when I discovered that they could only be worn on Sunday, so I transferred my enthusiasm to the cardboard box. I had an idea.

"I'll trade you scraps for your coloured gelatine paper," I said to Madge. My scraps were new and had not yet been pulled apart because my scrapbook was full and it would be Christmas before I got another one.

"How much do you want?" she said. "I'll have to see the scraps first." We struck a fair deal, advised by Babs and Betty. I climbed on the chair and took my shoe-box from the kitchen press. My sisters abandoned their scraps and their comics and crowded around me at the end of the kitchen table. Mam was reluctant to let us have the scissors as she maintained that it wouldn't cut butter if she allowed us cut paper with it, but in the end she relented, particularly as this was turning into a communal effort that would keep us all quiet until bedtime.

I had a collection of pictures and could choose between a picture of Shirley Temple, which I had exchanged silver paper for in school, or one of Deanna Durban looking heavenward, but the one I liked best was a picture of a little girl standing beside a duck-pond. I had saved it from a box of chocolates the previous Easter and I proceeded now to cut it to size. My mother produced a saucer of flour-and-water paste and I carefully pasted my picture on the inside of the box at a short end. I had hoarded coloured silver paper from my cousin's cigarette packets and Easter-egg wrapping, and sticking this along the inside walls of the box was the hardest part of the operation, because the paste bubbled in spots.

Then I cut a viewing oblong at the other short end, opposite the picture, while Betty and Tess jabbed holes in the lid of the box. The lid with its rows of holes was firmly placed back on the box.

"We'll have to sort the colours for the lights into a proper order." Babs always wanted things in proper order.

"Whose Pin-to-see-the-Show is it anyway?" I asked her.

"Easy, easy," my mother said. "Let's all work it out. What about the brightest colours at the front, like in the cinema. The yellows and oranges will be near the screen and they'll brighten it up."

"Then I want to put different colours in all the rest of the holes, so that they'll look like a rainbow," I said. Madge had given me red, orange, green and blue gelatine paper, and the trick was to wrap a coloured paper around your finger and insert it carefully into the hole and ever so gently take back the finger. Through the oblong viewer at the end of the box, the pieces of coloured paper looked like lightbulbs.

It was ready. Everybody was allowed have a go, and while they looked through the viewer I passed my hand backwards and forwards over the box top, dimming and brightening the lights, which winked and blinked on my cinema screen.

The next day the audience lined up at our back gate after school. The fee expected was a jelly-baby, a honey-bee toffee or a Nancy ball, but nobody was turned away even if they did not have the price of admission. It didn't really matter. When the showing was over, we all sat down around the Show and held a party.

Going to see the Miser's house was an adventure to be indulged in when ordinary games got boring. The Miser did not live near us, nor was he in the path of our message-carrying chores. He lived in a dull row of houses at the back of the farms across Mooney's field. When we came to the Miser's we stopped on the corner opposite his house and stared.

"I dare ye run past it."

"No I won't." This was one dare I would pass up. I might risk Mad Mary because I could out-run her, but I was not sure I would escape the Miser's long fingernails which would reach out and pull me into the dark grey house. The house was shabby and forbidding, its lace curtains dirty and torn. Weeds grew up the side of the garden path and the gate was rusted and closed tight.

"Does anybody know what he looks like?"

"He has long white hair and a long white beard and he has never cut his nails. They're like an eagle's claws, and when he grabs little children, they're never seen again."

A twitch of the curtain sent us scuttling to the end of the street.

"The cobwebs in the rooms are as high as the ceiling, and he never, never opens the door to anyone – not even the gas-man nor the electricity nor the coal-man."

"How does the Miser get his food if he doesn't come out of his house and if nobody goes in?"

My father lowered the evening paper. "Who says he's a miser? He's probably just a lonely old man who's afraid of the likes of you and me and only comes out when its dark. Of course he comes out to buy his food, don't be silly."

"Is it true that he has sacks of gold standing in his kitchen, and there's a big black cat would scrawb your eyes out if ye tried to take any of it?"

"Oh, God, child, what'll we do with ye? Your imagination is as good as a physic to a fool. Somebody's been filling your head with stories. Will ye sit down there like a good girl and read me this paper. I'll have to go to the Eye-man to get these glasses changed."

I didn't really believe him that his glasses needed changing; he just wanted to get me off the subject of the Miser and he succeeded.

We whiled away the winter nights when it was too wet to go out, making cats' cradles from pieces of string, crossing and weaving them around our fingers to see who could make the most intricate patterns. We plaited hairbands and bracelets from folded gelatine and silver papers and proudly wore them to school next morning.

January was the one month in the year when we were allowed stay out after dark. Heavy frosts and snow could sometimes turn the roads into an icy fairyland, and we set up rival slides on the footpaths and often in the middle of the street. There was never any traffic on our roads after dark and adults could be depended upon to walk with caution. There were enough children around to see that they did!

"It's very dark out there," my father warned as he let us out the door. "Check on each other all the time and don't stray down the road or out into Cork Street. Stay together and you'll be safe." We were never quite sure what he meant. He looked at us and repeated the warning.

"And remember," he said, "there are nasty people around who would like to harm little children, so stay together and don't talk to strangers." We solemnly nodded at him and to each other and knew that we would see him check on us constantly from the front door.

Our mother was a tougher proposition sometimes. "No, you're not moving out of here until you have your gaiters on." Betty, Tess and I stood looking at her as she barred our way. "It's either Russian boots or gaiters, so make up your minds." A severe frost was spitting its tiny barbs through the air and we could hear the fun starting outside. We had worn our Russian boots to school, but behind my mother's back we had changed into our leather shoes – with their thick soles, they were ideal for sliding. Russian boots would "gap" the slide and the others would stop us using it. My mother knew this, too.

"Nobody else wears gaiters," I pleaded.

"Nobody else was near to death's door with pneumonia," she retorted.

"It looks as if I'll be living with pneumonia for the rest of my days," I muttered under my breath.

We searched for the gaiters, which I had hidden in the recess under the stairs, and sat down reluctantly to put them on. They were made from a horrible muddy-brown felt material and were anchored by an elastic strap under the shoe. Button-ing them up around the ankle was easy but buttoning them over the calf and up to the knee gave us a lot of trouble. When we had battled successfully to put them on, we found them warm and snug, but I wasn't going to admit that. I stood up, my face purple with exertion, ready to go out and play.

Every child on the roads became pantomime-mad just after Christmas. Budding child stars and tap-dancing prodigies danced up and down the paths, but in our house we were Irish dancers and tap-dancing was regarded as alien. However, that did not stop us from dancing and swinging and tapping our way to stardom on the lino floor for my mother and father after we had been to the pantomime matinee. For weeks afterwards we learned and sang the pantomime songs, but all our talent simply could not persuade my father to put loose steel clips on the toes of our shoes.

"I'd love, I'd *really* love to learn fancy dancing. Can I?"

"No. You have your Irish dancing."

Oh, well. I thought I'd have another try. Nothing ventured, nothing gained.

"When can I have taps on my shoes? I could treble a hornpipe a lot better if I had."

"Maybe next year, maybe never."

The shoes remained as they were, with steel tips on the heels and none on the toes. But if my mother and father had plans for us other than tap-dancing our way through life, that was not going to stop me from planning my own artistic career. There never was a better time than after the pantomimes when we were all fired with theatre enthusiasm.

"Can I be principal boy?" Maddy's brother wanted a part. We had managed to rope in Jennie's, Ann's and Maddy's brothers to be doormen, curtain-pullers, prompters and furniture carriers, but we had never intended that they would do any of the acting. They wouldn't stay serious for two minutes.

"No, because the principal boy has to be a girl." As I meant to play all principal boy parts myself, that was that. Ann was Cinderella because she could sing; at least she sang solo in school. Maddy was Buttons. Jennie was the Fairy Godmother because she wanted a part where she did not have a lot to do. Joan and Betty were the Ugly Sisters because Joan's mother said she could make their wigs out of old wool. The boys carried the furniture, which we called stones, from the end of the play-yard and the Back of the Pipes to build a roofless theatre, and for that they got free entry to the Show. As it was not possible to hang a curtain in thin air, we appointed a Boss who announced when the curtain was up and when it came down. The audience was expected to use its imagination, and if they couldn't, well, that was their loss, and maybe they should be off playing ball.

Some of the boys not included in our select cast or engaged as helpers, pelted us with stones or shouted rude remarks at the stage. At these times we resorted to the Terrace, a cul-de-sac with an open space at the top where the householders hung out their washing. The entrance to the Terrace was narrow and could be held against invaders. Here we played our Prince Charmings and fairy Princesses, kicked our heights like the girls in the choruses, and tried to do the splits and the cake-walk, but flapping and flowing clothes-lines eventually defeated the success of this venture and we had to move on.

Play-acting in the open air was dependent on the weather, and with dark skies again threatening our production of *Cinderella* we had to think hard about finding our own theatre. I came up with the ideal place. Beside our playground was a big field and in the far corner was a store belonging to the Frigidaire factory. It had a covered-in entrance where the lorries loaded, and on the days when the factory was closed, this would be just perfect for staging our theatricals. We peered through the railings which divided our playground from the factory field. There was a break where one of the upright bars was missing, and so, too, was the watchman. Jennie, Maddy, Joan and I slid through and crept up to the car-port. It was beautiful; there was a roof and three walls. There were even wooden beams. We thought we could borrow some curtains and nail them up. We began to plan butter-box seating.

On the following Monday after school the four of us watched the men loading the lorries. Now was the time to act. We decided we would approach the manager and tell him we only wanted to use the empty space at weekends when they weren't using it. It was really very simple. We eased our bodies through the narrow railing again and walked bravely through the stinging nettles and long grass. We were halfway across the field when we heard the yell:

"You kids there; get to hell outa here. I'll skelp the daylights outa ye if I catch ye here again!"

The upraised voice and waving arms and the surprised looks of the men had us racing and falling over each other until we reached the playground gate. We re-grouped, but the case was lost. Next day there was an old man at the space in the railings and we watched silently as he fitted and inserted an iron bar, our dreams of a playhouse fading with each blow of the heavy hammer.

We searched the neighbourhood for likely venues. We seriously considered asking the managers of the two local cinemas for permission to use their empty foyers when the cinemas were closed during the day, but the cleaners wagged long fingers at us and chased us with wet brooms. Then one day when the rain drizzled across the playground and the washing at the top of the Terrace dripped dismally down on us, we sought shelter to hatch our further plans in one of the side entrances of the Rialto cinema. We huddled despondently on the porch, a drooping band of budding artistes. But suddenly our spirits lifted, and in a flash of imagination that little porch became our theatre. For one short afternoon at the Rialto we were Judy Garland singing "Over the Rainbow", the Royalettes swinging our legs, Conny Ryan's dancing babies tapping our way to fame, and each one of us a Shirley Temple or a Jane Withers or a Mickey Rooney. The cinema behind us was on Broadway, the grubby lollipop faces of the kids on the street our adoring fans, and the smoking chimneys of the dreary houses our rainbows to stardom.

# War Clouds Over Dublin

F OR DAYS MY father had stayed close to the wireless in the
parlour, tuning it up and down the waveband and
nearly driving my mother mad.

Boom, boom, boom, boom, boom...

Proudly the note of the trumpet is sounding,

Loudly the war-cries arise on the gale.

Never had Radio Athlone's signature tune seemed more
appropriate as we listened to the news coming from the little
wireless on the table.

"War clouds are gathering over Europe," intoned the
solemn voice of the announcer. It was Sunday, 3 September
1939. The war clouds had already prevented us from going to
ten o'clock Mass in Donore Avenue, I thought, because the
skies had opened and rain had bucketed down from early
morning. Europe, however, was very far away, much further
than England according to my atlas.

"Are the war clouds raining down on us?" I asked my father.

"Don't be silly," he reassured me as we got ready for last
Mass. "The war is far away. It will never touch us. The rain is
only a local thunderstorm which will be gone by afternoon."

During the Mass I watched the dullness of the stained-glass
windows lighten and the reds and greens and purples come

alive as the sun split through the clouds and slanted in ghostly rays across the priest's green and gold vestments, but just as they did, the priest interrupted the ceremony and told the congregation that Britain was now at war with Germany. My imagination took flight. I heard the Latin words, "*qui cum patre et filio simul adoratur, et conglorificatur*" as "Poland, Czechoslovakia, Albania" – names which had been tumbling out of the wireless for the past few weeks.

Outside the chapel everything was normal except for the bare-footed newsboys running with their sheaves of "stop-press". From that day until the end of the war, their piercing cries and the placards outside each small huxter's shop, with loud black-lettered notices announcing each new move of the war, gave a sense of urgency to our everyday lives.

For a while life did not change much. Ugly concrete air-raid shelters were built at various points along the streets, long oblong buildings without rhyme or reason we thought, certain we would never need them. But the day we were measured for gas-masks in the Boys' National School in Rialto was frightening. The tin snout was fastened around our heads with wide straps, and the smell of rubber was suffocating. I don't remember anyone protesting. Though we were all frightened, we were beginning to accept that this war, although it was happening as far away as England, was our war, too. There was a sense of importance in carrying home the cardboard box containing the mask.

"What d'ye think you're doin' with that?" My mother surveyed the box beside me the next morning as I ate my breakfast.

"We might get bombed on the way to school."

"And the Liffey'll run dry on its way to the sea. Leave that behind you. We'll know soon enough when we're going to be bombed."

"But the ARP man said..."

"The ARP man is full of his own importance. Trust the likes of him to give his sense to a child. The war'll not get within an ass's roar of us. Eat your breakfast and get off to school."

The streets were full of important-looking people these days. Men we would have walked past without noticing before now sported uniforms and tin-hats and heavy-looking glass bottles slung in cases at their waists. Girls swaggered about in Red Cross uniforms. My mother and father attended meetings where they learned emergency first-aid and were given talks on how to camouflage and best protect their homes. Bandages, packets of boric lint and disinfectant were loaded into a tin box which sat on the kitchen window.

My mother took herself off to Frawley's in Thomas Street to buy material for black-out curtains. Every window was blacked out from early evening and busybody Air-Raid Precautions men knocked on people's doors if a chink of light showed through the curtains. Dublin Corporation sent men around to put hoods on all the streetlamps, so that instead of spreading out and upwards, the light shone in pools on the pavement. We never really believed that the pilots who flew the bombers could see the chinks of light peeping from someone's window, but we knew they were around when we saw the searchlights from Griffith and Collins Barracks slicing the night sky.

Then one night we heard a bomber flying low over our street. Babs and I hunched in the little cubby-hole under the stairs, listening to the heavy drone of the engine as the plane seemed to circle, getting lower and lower. Madge, Betty and Tess were under the kitchen table while my mother moved anxiously about, offering us words of reassurance. Nance lay fast asleep upstairs. My father, in common with all the men on the streets around, stood silent watch at the darkened doorway, craning his head to the sky. When the bang came, my mother sprang for the stairs.

"Jesus, Mary and Joseph – the child!" she cried as she swept the front door closed, catapulting my father down the steps. He hammered on the door to be let in. We mumbled prayers as we heard the sounds of anti-aircraft guns in the distance, the screeching of police cars and ambulances, and waited for the reassuring sound of the "all-clear". Later we learned that bombs had been dropped near the Jewish Synagogue on the South Circular Road. After that, air-raid precautions were stepped up.

To help the people in the war, and for other good causes, children's fancy dress fêtes were held to raise money for the Red Cross.

"You can go as a soldier," my mother said to me, "and Betty can be your nurse." My mother put her heart and soul into these dressing-up sessions. I was fitted out in an old pair of my father's pants, its legs lopped off and pulled into folds at the waist. My hand, head and right eye were swathed in torn strips of sheeting and liberally spattered with red ink. My left arm was slung in a sling and an old school blouse was wiped with wet ash from the stove to give it an authentically battle-torn look. Betty, with her curly hair and pretty face, had the better part. My mother dressed her in a blue calico dress over which she wore a white pinny with a large red cross stitched with red ribbon. She had great difficulty in holding the three-cornered head-dress in place as it kept slipping off her unruly curls.

When we got to the local hall, our hearts sank. Every second child was dressed as a nurse, and there was a fair spinkling of crutches and broken arms.

"We'll enter you as 'the most original pair'," my mother

said. "But you'll have to act the part. It's your only chance."

When our turn came to parade before the judges, I leaned on Betty's arm and limped slowly around the circle. My groaning and moaning could be heard in the next room. We stopped at strategic points in front of the judges, while Betty mopped my brow and gave me sips of water from the bottle she carried. We won – whether for the costumes or the acting we never knew – but we carried home a brown biscuit barrel topped with a silver lid in triumph.

The Emergency, as the war was called in Ireland, was to remain for the rest of my childhood and into my growing up. As the war progressed, shortages developed, and everyone was issued with ration-books, whose coupons could be used to purchase butter, tea and sugar. You registered your ration books with whatever grocer you wished, and the grocer in his turn informed the suppliers how many customers he had, so that he would receive the right amount of goods. The ration of tea was two ounces a week per person at first, but as the war went on and supplies became scarcer, the amount dropped to one ounce and then finally it became half an ounce per person. The beautiful fluffy white bread which was the mainstay of every Dublin home turned a light brown, and more brown flour was added until it became the hated black bread of the Emergency, quick to sour and grow stale. Dublin people envied the fact that in Belfast and England white bread could still be bought. Parodies on the wartime songs which had crossed the Irish Sea on the wireless were popular, and none more so than the one which went:

Bless 'em all, bless 'em all,
Bless all who sit in the Dáil;
Bless de Valera and Sean McEntee
For giving us brown bread and two ounces of tea.
But they took back an ounce and a half

And gave it to poor oul' Belfast,
And they'll get no promotion this side of the ocean
So cheer up, me lads, bless 'em all.

Clothes, too, were rationed and a great black market trade was set up buying and selling clothing coupons, especially from families which might not have the money to use all the coupons they were allocated. Great lumps of yellow and red Sunlight and carbolic soap were hoarded and doled out with strict instructions to use it sparingly. Scraps of soap were collected in jam-jars and soaked in water to make a glutinous mess which could be used to wash clothes.

In school, jotters became the despair of our teachers. When our good writing copies began to sprout slivers of straw along the sides of the pages, there were wails of "The paper's all blotting, Sister." The pen would go through the paper, and we had to resort to pencils to practise writing. The purple fraughan berries which we used to collect in the woods above Aughrim were now being used to make ink.

Life became peppered with exciting cries which announced black market tea in the Barn and white flour in a shop in Meath Street.

"Keep your eyes peeled and your ears wide open," was dinned into our ears every morning as we set out for school. "If you see a queue, ask what it's about and then come home fast." Spotting a queue had its disadvantages, because you were usually sent back to join it with money in your fist for whatever was selling and strict instructions as to how much was to be paid for it. Order had suddenly come into our lives. Nobody had ever queued before – at bus-stops and tram-stops the strongest and most nimble always won the battle – but now we stood in docile lines everywhere. Queuing became a way of life.

My mother foraged and hoarded and stored and shared

with those less thrifty when the need arose. Teapots stewed until every last drop was extracted; tea leaves were dried and re-used again. Tea, which had cost from half-a-crown to three shillings for a pound, suddenly rose to £1 per pound on the black market. My mother tried switching to cocoa, but that too disappeared as chocolate beans became scarce.

"What's that awful smell?" We had come in from school and found mother stewing something on the gas cooker.

"It's shell cocoa," she said. "It's new in the shops and sup-posed to be very good." We were wary of anything that was supposed to be good for us, and we handed her back our cups, the cocoa untouched.

Gas for cooking and heating the little gas-fires in the bed-rooms became severely rationed. Cooking could only be done at certain times and these did not always coincide with family meals. Mothers swore that the gas-company altered the times deliberately to conserve gas, and they were kept on their toes watching the gas-time routines, or else they resorted to the glimmer. When the gas was turned off in an area, gas re-mained in the pipes for a while and a small flame could be coaxed from it. Stern warnings were issued about the danger of using the glimmer, as it was called, and the gas-company sent inspectors around to check for suspiciously warm kettles or burners. As a result, every stranger on a bicycle became a target of suspicion.

"Are you the glimmer man, Mister?" If he was, his quest was in vain because every house was already warned of his pres-ence. Curtains would twitch as he passed until, knowing the battle was lost, the glimmer man pedalled wearily away.

But some alternative form of cooking had to be found; needs must when the devil drives, as my father put it. Suddenly my mother's store of biscuit tins came into their own. Sawdust fires had been suggested to households as an alternative way of cooking, and the tins would make ideal braziers.

"Every shoulder to the plough," my father said as he hoisted a bag of sawdust from the saw-mills in Thomas Street. He measured the sawdust into a biscuit tin and pressed it into a solid cake. A hole in the centre allowed air to circulate, and when it was set alight the sawdust smouldered with a gentle heat which cooked a stew slowly or simmered potatoes and cabbage. If it became too frisky and started to blaze it could be damped down with cold water.

The fire was the heart of every home in winter, but suddenly coal was hard to come by. Slack and coal-dust, which would have been disdained in better times, was dredged up from coal-merchants' yards and used to bank up the fire. We patted and shaped slack and cement into coal-blocks in our back-garden. Wet slack wrapped in parcels of newspapers dried into a solid mass which hissed and spluttered and damped the fire down, only to reward us an hour later with a solid glow of cinders. The cinders were carefully sorted from the ashes the following morning, wiped clean of dust and offered up to the fire again that evening.

Then turf arrived in Dublin. Mountains of it appeared in the Phoenix Park and our outings to the People's Gardens were suspended as we trudged instead to look at the rows piling up on both sides of every road in the park. Having watched our cousins cut and foot and stack turf during the summer in County Wicklow, the new fuel was no surprise to us, but it was to most Dubliners.

"In the name of God, man, you don't expect me to light the fire with that muck. It's wet, wringing wet!"

The bell-man who usually sold coal and sticks to his customers had pulled his cart into Eugene Street, and the women were giving him a hard time. I stopped to watch.

"What d'ye want me to do about it, Ma'am; put it under me oxter and squeeze it? That's the best turf this side of the Dublin mountains."

"Aye. And by the looks of it, it swam every river on the way."

The turf was always wet. It was covered only by canvas strips at the top of the bank but was otherwise open to the elements. "They hose it to keep it damp, too, for fear of fire," my father added as we wandered down the brown aisles, past the Goff Monument in the Phoenix Park.

"Ye can't take your eyes off them for one minute," a soldier patrolling the rows told us, his voice at a pitch of frustration. "Some of them chis2lers would rob their own grannies." Then he set off in hot pursuit of two youngsters lugging a sackful of sods which they had nicked from the foot of the pile.

MY MOTHER USED the war for her own ends.

"What's up?"

"Nothing's up."

"Something must be up. What's wrong with Daddy?" My father was pacing up and down the kitchen floor, his hands behind his back, eyes bent on the floor.

"Your daddy is thinking of joining the army."

"Which army?"

"The British army." I could see my mother's eyes on me, weighing up how I was taking it.

"Going to the war?"

"Hmm."

"You're not going to the war. You're not, you're not, you're not." I began banging my father's legs until he caught me and lifted me high in the air.

"We're only letting on," he said as he lowered me to the

floor. "Sure nobody'd have me. But we've got something important to tell you."

"You won't be gettin' any toys for Christmas this year. Well," my mother hesitated, "you see we really want to tell you that there's no Santa Claus. You're a big girl now. You'll be getting a new pleated skirt for Christmas, for your Christmas present."

I didn't care at that minute if every Santa Claus and Daddy Christmas were at the bottom of the sea. I had been a big girl for ages and I was well aware that Santa Claus was only for babies. I had known all that for a very long time.

"It stands to reason," Jennie had argued one day coming home from school. "How could any Santa Claus come down our chimney, the fires are always lighting. And how could any Santa Claus bring all the things children ask for, to every one of them?"

"But you can't say that you don't believe or you'll get nothin'."

Jennie nodded her head in agreement. "The day you say you've stopped believing is the day the presents stop."

The thought of no more *Dandy* and *Beano* annuals, not to mention Lord Snooty and his pals, Our Gang and Keyhole Kate, or jigsaw puzzles and cut-out dolls with different outfits, had kept us cagey for a long while. It suited us to ignore the nods and winks and whispering of those who would enlighten us if we choose to let them. In our house Santa Claus had to be kept alive for Betty, Tess and Nance, who still believed in Santa's magic.

Casting off my Santa Claus years lost its trauma in the relief of knowing that my father was not on his way to join any army, Irish or British. I did not want to become like the little boy in the song which we heard every Christmas:

In the streets he envies all those lucky boys,

Then wanders home to last year's broken toys.
I'm so sorry for that laddie, he hasn't got a daddy.
He's the little boy that Santa Claus forgot.

As Christmas approached, wooden toys began to fill the
shops, as tin, paint and metal-based material became scarce.
The biggest worry for our mothers, though, was how to produce a decent Christmas pudding. Making the pudding was
an obligation of honour, and it was made in all homes on the
morning of Christmas Eve. The war was a challenge to produce a pudding against all the odds.

"I heard tell from a woman over opposite," a neighbour told
my mother, "that there's boxes of muscatels in Meath Street."
My mother had gone by the time we came home from school:
it was never wise to wait. The muscatel raisin was a big juicy
wodge of fruit filled with brown stones which had to be exca-
vated before the business of the pudding was undertaken.
This was a job for everybody, and we gathered around the
bowl of exotic fruit on the kitchen table, slitting, cutting and
extracting. My mother had also acquired a loaf of white bread
from England, from her cousin whose husband worked on
the Guinness boats. The bread was soaked overnight, and
then her store of fruit peel was taken out, sugar added with
plenty of nutmeg and mixed spice, and my mother, her arms
bare to the elbow, squeezed the whole mass through her fingers. Finally she poured in the all important bottle of stout,
and we each took a turn at stirring the mixture. With the
wooden spoon in my hand, I closed my eyes tight and
wished, but there were so many things to wish for I got confused and blinked them open again.

"You've lost your wish." Betty was at my elbow.

"How do you know?" I pushed her away.

"Because I didn't see your lips move," she said, "and you
have to say it inside very clearly or the wish won't come true."

"Have another go," my mother said, "and try and concentrate."

I concentrated all right this time but I knew I had lost my wish anyway. There was no way I was going to get a two-wheeled bicycle for Christmas.

When my mother was satisfied that the mixture was just right, she spread the white blay calico pudding cloth on the kitchen table, scooped up the pudding with her sticky hands and laid it on the cloth, carefully gathering the ragged corners into pleats which she tied with string. Then she lowered it gently into the steaming pot of boiling water and it gently simmered its way through Christmas Eve.

On Christmas morning the pudding came into its own. "Ye can't leave the house without a taste of puddin'," our mother or father would insist as neighbours and relations called. Nobody did. "Ye'll wash it down with a drop of port or maybe a half-one." But more often than not it was a glass of porter which was placed on the tray beside the slice of pudding.

When the visitation of neighbours and cousins was finished on Christmas morning and the adults were slightly merry, hall-doors were closed against the world and families settled down for Christmas Day. The goose, which Aunt Nanny had sent on the train from Aughrim, cooked slowly in the gas oven in the kitchen. We read our annuals, did jig-saws, played snakes-and-ladders and draughts in the afternoon, and then the adults rested. It was a long time since the six-o'clock Mass that morning and my father dozed in his chair, but we shook him awake to listen to "Hospital Requests" from the Children's Hospital in Cappagh. This he would never miss. The voices of the children, far from home and family, brought tears to his eyes, and I looked away embarrassed, seeking refuge in my cut-out dolls. As night closed in, we sat in the deepening shadow, the light from the open fire dancing across the gaudy paper-chains and Chinese lanterns, and the Christmas candle flickering.

The Christmas candle glowed in every window from dusk on Christmas Eve to welcome Mary and the Christ Child, house vying with house to see whose candle was lighted first. During the early years of the war it stood behind blacked-out windows, and then one awful year the long red candle, beacon of light to welcome the Holy Family on their journey, was no more. Wax had become another casualty of the war.

"I DON'T WANT to leave home and go to some old farm down the country." Maddy had never been further than the Ramparts on the Crumlin Road and the strand at Sandymount. We were sitting on the wall at the top of the Pipes, and we were all feeling down in the dumps. We had just seen the newsreels in the Leinster cinema showing the forlorn little faces of the evacuees on London's train platforms.

"You can't take all your clothes and things with you because there won't be room in the little cottages. You're only allowed to carry a few things." And we remembered the little attaché cases and the schoolbags on the cinema screen.

"And they won't let your father and mother come to see ye," Jennie chipped in, "because there'll be no trains and no buses, because there'll be no petrol."

"If there's no trains then how will they get us to the country?"

"Maybe we'll go in the army lorries." We remembered the army lorries from the bus strike when we boarded them at Dolphin's Barn and were transported to the end of the Coombe – a journey we never had any difficulty in undertaking on foot, but because it cost us nothing during the strike, we went along for the jaunt.

"That could be right," I nodded. There was talk of all the signposts around the country being taken down in case the Germans landed, so that they wouldn't know where they were. It stood to reason that our army would know where to bring the evacuee children: they had maps.

"It's all right for you," Jennie said, and everybody turned to look at me. "You have your cousins in the country and you can go to them." I wasn't too sure about that. I felt certain my mother would want all her chickens about her if war was threatening, and she would be a match for any evacuation officer if one ever tried to take us from her.

Young as I was, I understood that war was a dreadful thing and did horrible things to people. Like Damn the Weather with his cold-weather face, perpetually rubbing his hands as he shivered in his jacket winter and summer. "Sure the Lord love him, but he's a harmless poor cratur," people said. Damn the Weather looked neither to right nor left as he stamped his way up and down Dolphin's Barn, his thin face reddened and pinched, his hands burrowing under his armpits and then suddenly shaken loose as he shouted "Damn the Weather!" his eyes focused directly ahead, oblivious to all about him.

"Shell-shocked in the First World War."

"The Lord preserve us from another one."

I did not know much about the First World War, but now here we were in the middle of a second, and I was particularly worried about these things they called shells. Nobody seemed to know what they were, but they certainly could not have been the shells which my mother had for decoration in her front garden and which we put to our ears so as to hear the sea.

"D'ye think the Granny was in the war, too, and got shell-shocked?" We were holding the Granny tightly by the arms, one on each side of her. She wasn't our granny, but everyone called her that. She had a habit of wandering into our road to look for Jack. She grabbed us by the sleeve of our dresses and asked us if we had seen him. Who Jack was we didn't know, but her face brightened as we promised her we would find him and bring him back to her. We worried about her because some days she wandered aimlessly with no hat or coat on, and her eyes were anxious and distressed. We would take her back to her own part of the neighbourhood, stand her outside her family's door, knock and then run and stand at the corner to make sure that they took her in. We never minded doing this because we were helping an old lady and felt good about it, though it wasn't so easy if we were in a hurry. Our parents just shook their heads:

"Leave her alone; she'll come to no harm. She'll not wander far." And then for months on end we never saw her and we imagined she was locked in some room and could not get out to look for Jack. Just as we thought she must surely be dead, the little humped figure was back again, searching the streets.

So I hated this war. Surely, I thought to myself, whoever started it knows about the one-legged and one-armed men, the men with shell-shocked brains, and the old ladies who after all these years were still searching for their loved ones.

More and more now I wished hard and strong and lit candles in the chapel whenever I could afford it, for somebody to do something to that awful little man with the unreal moustache and the outstretched arm, the man who was responsible for it all. The one they called Hitler.

# A Little Learning

I T MAY HAVE been that the black-out curtains were on my
mind, but all around me I could see nothing but people
wearing dark clothes. Or perhaps it was because clothes
were becoming important to me: my first grown-up outfit
had been for Confirmation two years before, and now my
mother said I was getting too big to make more coats for me.
My winter coat was to be made by a dressmaker in
Clanbrassil Street. The colour of that coat was very much on
my mind.

"I wonder," I said to Jennie as we kicked the leaves before us
on our way from school. "I wonder what's the age you have to
be before they start tellin' you to wear dark clothes."

"Maybe the shops don't make bright clothes for grown-
ups."

"They do." I was pretty definite about this because we had a
distant relative we met on family occasions, and she wore
bright clothes. "I know somebody who wears bright red with
everything."

I loved to see her; she looked so bright and different from
our parents in their dull clothes, with their black, brown or
grey skirts and white or cream blouses. Hats were an exception sometimes; they had feathers or ribbons which were dis-

creetly moulded on to dark melton cloth in winter and straw in summer. In winter my mother also wore a fox-fur. I never asked if it had once been real; if it had, I didn't want to know. It had beady eyes, a bone-cold nose and sharp claws. I liked to stroke its silky fur because it sent a shiver up my back, but only if somebody was in the room and I knew then it would not snap at me. I loved the feel of the fox-fur's silk lining, but resisted all attempts to put it around my neck. When it lay flat across the seat of the kitchen chair while my mother dressed, its glinting amber eyes would follow me into the living-room as I edged past.

"It won't bite you," they said, but I wasn't so sure, and always gave it the benefit of the doubt. I would refuse to carry it to the bedroom unless somebody stayed at the bottom of the stairs, and then I would open the bedroom door as fast as I could, fling the fox-fur on to the end of my parents' bed, and bang the door behind me.

Neither Jennie's mother nor mine wore their clothes the length the nuns did. Their habits came down exactly to the tops of their buttoned boots.

"You never see their ankles." We had spotted two of them ahead of us, and stopped kicking the leaves.

The nuns always walked in twos, two heads bobbing together and, it seemed, two sets of feet moving in unison. We never saw a nun on her own outside the school or convent gates.

"You must see their ankles," Jennie said, "when they genuflect in the chapel."

"No, you don't. I've watched." And I had watched the graceful movements of head and hands. Down they went on one knee and then as they rose they took a fold of skirt and lifted it so it did not catch on their heel as they slipped into their seats. The fold of skirt was held only so high as to reveal the side piece of the boot but no more.

"I think they must practise it in the convent for hours on end; you know, down on one knee, skirt in hand, no ankle to show, one, two, three, one, two, three... They couldn't do it unless they practised it."

"I think I'd go mad if I had to wear black all the time." The colour of people's clothes was still on my mind next day as we polished the desks in preparation for one of Reverend Mother's visits.

"They wear a lot of white, too, near their faces, and it looks well on them," Joan objected as she tried to brasso around the inkwells. "It makes them look special and saintly and different."

"Will you girls hurry up and stop gostering; we'll never get done." The figure at the door looked anything but saintly. She was hot and flustered with her outside skirt caught up at the sides and her sleeves protected by check protectors which stretched from wrist to elbow, and wisps of brown hair were escaping at the sides of the wimple.

"She's got brown hair," giggled Joan.

"You'll be havin' white hair if she hears ye," I hissed. "Yes, Sister, we're just about finished."

"Proper English, girl. You're not 'just about finished'. You have finished, do you understand me, girl?"

When she had left, Jennie and I continued our discussion.

"Is there a difference in the convents, do ye think, like there is between the brothers and the priests?" We had already decided that the monks who wore sandals and no socks were the poor brothers who had no money, and the ones who had shoes and wore black suits with white back-to-front collars must all be priests, and we should accord them the respect they were due by saying "God bless you, Father" when they passed. After all, they might be carrying the Blessed Sacrament. Some of us might one day like to become nuns, and I wanted to be clear about all these distinctions. "Is there a difference?" I asked Jennie again.

"Oh, there is a difference." We turned to look at Carmel, who had volunteered the answer. She said she had an aunt who was a nun, but nobody really believed her. She had never been able to produce the aunt, who was always on the Missions somewhere, and so her claim was like saying you had an uncle who was a doctor. This could not happen, as we all knew, because you needed lots of money to become a doctor and doctors usually came from doctors' families. Priests and nuns rarely came from our families either.

"My mam says that you have to have pots of money to be a nun; it's called a dowry and if you haven't got a dowry then you become one of the other nuns and do the cleaning jobs and serve the nuns their meals."

"I heard that, too," Madge confirmed. Her aunt did some housekeeping for a priest. "They don't even kneel in the same part of the chapel and they can't sing in the choir; my aunt says the rules of the convent say they're not good enough, they're only the servants."

"I'm sure that's not true," I rounded on Madge. Becoming a nun mightn't be all that bad, and I had a sneaking suspicion that I might like to try it some day. "If I become a nun, I won't be anybody's servant," I said as I flounced out the classroom door.

"No, you'd want to be Reverend Mother, wouldn't you?" Madge flung at me as she raced passed me down the iron stairs.

"Stranger things have happened," I wanted to shout at her but she was gone.

When our school was founded by the Sisters of Mercy in the mid-1800s, it was supported by the dowries of the nuns and the generous subscriptions of their friends and families. I was very proud of my school – at least I was proud on most days. We were in awe of our teachers and nuns, and while we were in their care they cocooned and bullied and fashioned us for ten years of our lives – and then sent us forth at the raw age of fourteen years to fend for ourselves.

As I moved into my last years in school, I came up against one nun who never lost the opportunity of telling me what I was not – a patch on Madge, for whom she had a soft spot. She never lost an opportunity to put me in my place, as she saw it. One Monday morning I was proudly displaying a medal which I had won for Irish dancing the previous day, when into the classroom swept my tormentor. She propped herself against the table, flung back her veil and cocked her head in my direction.

"Showing off, Miss?" she said. "Come up and let us see what you have." Acid dripped from her voice and two pin-points of red showed on her cheeks. I advanced to the front of the class, wary of the sarcastic remarks she might fling at me. She held out her hand for my medal.

"And did you get your homework done while you were win-ning this medal, Miss?" I assured her that I had.

"And tell me, Miss, did you win this medal for the honour and glory of God?" It was a triumphant statement, her trump card. My mind flicked at the suddenness and the injustice of it. My medal did not deserve this. I gathered my wits together and said in a breathless voice, a little nervous as I fought my ground:

"Oh, yes, Sister." I gripped the desk in the front row, stub-bing my finger in the inkwell. "Yes, Sister," I said, "the com-petitions were held in aid of the Lourdes Invalid Fund."

From the age of twelve we were the seniors, the last three classes in the school, promoted to the classrooms on the edge of the school block high above the convent grounds. There was a sense of finality about those rooms, almost as if we were being pushed to the end of our school life. It was nearing time to go. Most of us had our Primary School Certificates safely in our pockets; we had finished the National School curriculum and were waiting for the day when the school doors would close behind us for the last time. I was not eager to be gone from school, but there were many who were and did not wait until their fourteenth birthday. In seventh and eighth classes we were a mixture of those who were too young or unwilling to leave, and those who had just moved up from sixth class. We thundered up an iron staircase on the outside of the building, legging it up the slippery surface with alarming speed, and in my final year I often stood on the square landing at the top and looked out over the city, wondering where I was going.

My one and only crush came in seventh class, when I was on the edge of emerging uncertainly into the adult world. I had come up unscathed through the whole of school without mooning over teachers or teacher students. This was different, and I was not alone. Sister Ita taught us for our last two years, and the class hung on her every word. She was tall and graceful and she had the bluest of blue eyes.

"I'm sure she was lovely before she entered," I ventured one day to Jennie as we watched Sister Ita walk across the yard to the convent gate. "She walks like a queen."

"You don't know any queens." Jennie was not given to mooning.

"I saw a queen on the newsreel in the Leinster."

"What queen?"

"How do I know?"

"Well if it's the queen I think ye saw, she doesn't look a bit like Sister Ita. She's small and dumpy."

Nobody, not even if she were queen of the whole world,

could look and walk like Sister Ita. And this nun was not soft; she was not in charge of forty young misses because she had a regal walk and glorious blue eyes. Those same eyes could cut like a blade.

Sister Ita knew my love of English composition and encouraged me to write little stories and read them for the class. Some of the descriptive passages in my stories I cheerfully lifted from *The Imeldist*, suffering pangs of guilt for days afterwards, but Sister Ita never batted an eyelid, never dropped a hint, never faulted me, never pointed out my stealing, but listened closely and encouraged. Yet even she could not save me on the day I was accused of blasphemy.

"Spring," Sister Ita said one afternoon, "we'll do a composition on spring for tonight's homework. Let's have some opening sentences." I hated this part of the English lesson; I could never think of opening sentences to say out loud on the spur of the moment.

"Spring is the first season of the year," a voice volunteered from the back of the class, and Sister Ita turned to write this wisdom on the blackboard.

While her back was turned one of the class hissed at me: "What did ye get for the second-last sum?" Our homework from the previous day was still not corrected. I fumbled for my jotter under the desk when Sister Ita turned slowly from the blackboard, her black veil dipping slightly as she inclined her head in my direction.

"Have you something to add to the opening sentence?" She was nobody's fool. "Yes, Miss: let us hear what you have to say on the subject of spring." I struggled uneasily to my feet, kicking over my milkbottle which had rolled out of my schoolbag. "Well?" she said, her head to one side.

I wanted to say that spring was clean and fresh and green, but I couldn't. I wanted to say that spring had cornflower blue eyes like hers, and rain-washed skies, but the class would have rocked with laughter. I looked at her pleadingly. I could think of plenty of opening sentences at home but not in front of this lot. I looked despairingly through the window and could see all the signs of spring, the maid in the convent garden shaking out the mats and the old gardener bending double over the flower-beds. I could smell the scents of spring through the open window – the clammy, sticky smell of Wills' tobacco factory which always gave me a headache, and the horrible gluey smell from Keeffe's the knackers. These were the things I would put in my composition when I was writing it at home, but I couldn't share this with the class. I was near to tears.

"Come on, child," she said gently, "just a simple little sentence." But it was too late. The door from the next classroom opened and the head-nun walked in on one of her visitations. The class rose to its feet.

*"Dia dhuit, a Shiúr,"* we chanted, and I sat down thankfully with the rest. But I was not going to get relief just yet.

"Continue with the class. You, girl," she said, pointing at me, "why were you standing up? Finish what you were saying." Sister Magdalen rattled her keys as Sister Ita explained about the composition. I stood up again. I could see Sister Ita's eyes pleading with me from behind the head-nun's back.

"Hurry up, child," Sister Magdalen fussed, "let us hear your masterpiece – you're taking long enough over it."

Something I had read the evening before flashed in my head. I did not stop to think.

"Arise, my love, my dove, my beautiful one and come, for the winter... " I stumbled as I tried to remember the words, "the winter is over and gone and spring has appeared in our land." I had thought it the most beautiful thing I had ever read, and it would make a great opening for my composition.

Sister Magdalen thought otherwise. I saw Sister Ita's eyes open wide in astonishment, but Sister Magdalen's mouth fell fully two inches. The class sniggered; nobody ever mentioned love, never.

"Silence, girls!" Sister Magdalen roared. "Where did you find that, Miss?"

"I read it in the *Messenger* when we got it yesterday, Sister," I said.

"Blasphemy," she stuttered, "blasphemy, pure and simple. What makes you think you can use the sacred words of Scripture in your composition, child?" The class fell quiet. Obviously Sister Magdalen considered I had done very wrong. I was confused and slightly defiant, but certain that I had done nothing wrong.

"But I thought it would be all right if it was in the *Messenger*, Sister," I ventured.

"You thought. You thought, Miss, did you?" she thundered. "You can't even think of a simple sentence. The next thing we know you'll be taking the Lord's name in vain in your compositions." Turning to Sister Ita she said:

"Let this child stay in during her lunch-hour and write the first verse of that Psalm ten times. If it's not finished at the end of lunchtime, she'll finish it at home, and let her bring it to me in the morning, and we'll see what's to be done about this."

I stayed in the empty classroom copying out the lines, and I finished them at home that night. Betty and Tess brought the story of my new fame home, and my mother, torn between her child and the nun's accusation of blasphemy, did not know what to think.

"Leave well enough alone," my father counselled. "Let's see what happens."

Nothing happened. Next morning I presented myself and

my copy-book at Sister Magdalen's office. I was too frightened to say a word. She looked at me as if she were about to say something, but changed her mind and ordered me to my class. She did not look at my lines.

At the end of the morning class Sister Ita called me to stay back. She handed me her books to carry to the convent gate and took an orange from the worn dusty pocket of her habit and placed it in my hands. Suddenly it was spring.

READING WAS IMPORTANT in our house. Comics were considered a luxury – money was needed for more important things than buying the *Dandy* and the *Beano*, though we traded marbles, sweets and help with homework with those who seemed to have comics as if by right. My father and mother encouraged us to read the newspapers out loud to them. My father would scan the *Evening Mail* or the *Herald* for an appropriate piece and sit back with his eyes closed while we struggled through the report.

My eldest sister, Madge, was top of her class at sums and geography, and her practical common sense was a great help to my mother. Babs was a reader and a dreamer. In the nuns' eyes, being a reader was the more important of the two. It set you apart, and it had to mean that you were good at everything else; if you were good at reading English, you must be good at reading Irish, and Latin would come easily, too. As a result, Babs got away with murder. The readers, because of their supposed intelligence, were sent to take charge of a class when a teacher was absent or, as in Babs' case, as a way of grooming a senior to set her sights on becoming a teacher. But I became a reader simply because I was inquisitive. I was not a dreamer; I just liked reading books.

My appetite for books had been sharpened in fourth class. Our new English reader was the story of a lone Indian named

Red Cloud. Up to this we had read stories about mythical Mammys and Daddys who worked in well-appointed kitchens and had gardens full of beautiful flowers which bore no resemblance to my mother's wallflowers and pansies. We read poems by Joseph Mary Plunkett and learned how much William Butler Yeats loved the Irish peasantry. But *Red Cloud* was just one long story from cover to cover. I couldn't believe it. I flew home from school, raced through my homework, and curled up on the kitchen chair, my legs tucked under me. I had a whole book to read, with chapters and headings, a beginning, a middle and an end, and I read until my mother took the book from me, declaring that I'd make myself blind. Even so, I had finished *Red Cloud* before the class got a third of the way through it in the reading-out-loud sessions where we all stood in a wide circle and took turns at reading.

Besides our textbooks we were given copies of *The Imeldist*, the *Sacred Heart Messenger* and the *Far East* to read, but we had no library in the school. I read everything I could lay my hands on from cover to cover, and in sixth class I was handed my card for the Public Library in Thomas Street.

Beyond the glass-panelled door with its huge notice – SILENCE – was a musty world of mysterious delight and adventure. With its closed blinds and dark interior, the library became a refuge from the heat of the city's pavements in summer, and in winter it was a place of warmth and security, its windows shuttered and an open fire sending shadows darting among the brown bookcases. We tiptoed around as if on eggshells, and if we conferred too long or too loudly over our books, Tim the librarian would stop indexing cards or stamping books and warn us to be quiet.

We were allowed two tickets, one for fiction, the other non-fiction, but nobody used the non-fiction ticket. Who wanted to read about somebody else's life or a journey up the Amazon or Butler's *Lives of the Saints?* I thought it was time somebody took this library system on, and I decided to try to borrow a second storybook.

"*Dimsie – Headgirl!* That's not a work of non-fiction!" Tim said scathingly. "Put it back!" he commanded in his strong country accent, and he watched me as I put the coveted book back on the shelves – there was no way I could sneak it out.

Row upon row of dull green- and brown-backed books were arranged in strict alphabetical order, and we made our way slowly along the bookshelves, searching for girls' books. It never crossed our minds that we could take out boys' books, and in turn any boy caught reading a girls' book would be branded a sissy. My mother and father trusted the library to make sure we read nothing unsuitable. There was no guidance from school; the nuns were glad we were reading, but never suggested books to us. So we learned from one another and ended up with the Abbey Girls, the Chalet School, the Daphne and Dimsie Maitland books, *What Katy Did* and did not do: all schoolgirl adventure stories set in posh boarding schools somewhere in the English countryside. We lapped up the paper-chases and the midnight feasts in the dorms and girls who adored their prefects and aimed to become headgirls. There was always a *Mamselle* who was a dreadful French teacher and the Games Mistress who stuck her chin out and loped along like an antelope and was a jolly good sort. Later came the Pollyanna books, and later still the light romances of Annie M.P. Smithson.

Not in our wildest imagination would we ever become like the girls in the storybooks. Theirs was a different world. The nearest we would come to it was to see the girls in the college on the Crumlin Road or the School for Young Ladies in the Coombe, where they wore smartly pressed gymslips, heavily pleated, with trailing sashes, startlingly white blouses, long blazers and crested berets, and they carried tennis racquets and hockey sticks.

I was the only serious reader among my friends and so it was up to me to plan any unusual games which I might read about. I read a description of a paper-chasein one of the Abbey Girls books and we laid our plans. Our first job was to gather as much newspaper as we could, but newspapers were a precious resource, carefully stored away and used for polishing windows, laying on the floor after it had been washed, or rolled up tightly to make fire-lighters. When we got past this first hurdle, I borrowed Tess's satchel, although she was unwilling to part with it, particularly as I told her that her legs were too short to join in the chase. We filled it with carefully torn scraps of paper and we drew lots as to who would be hares and who would be hounds.

"The hares will have to leg it as fast as they can up Cork Street," I said, and as organiser I intended to be one of the hares. "Give us odds of five minutes and then start after us."

Five minutes was three hundred seconds counted slowly – nobody owned a wrist-watch. We hares set out, dribbling our bits of paper as we raced up Cork Street, along Dolphin's Barn and back down the Pipes, making little detours to throw the hounds off the scent. But the hounds never even found the scent. How could they? Our scrappy bits of paper tangled with bigger scraps – cigarette packets, wrapping paper and all the flotsam of a busy street strewn about by horses' feet, bicycles and buses. Sadly we trailed home. I had ignored the fact that in the storybooks the trail was set over acres of green parkland and rolling downs.

"That's a stupid game," my friends said.

I was nearly inclined to agree, but I was not beaten yet. "It's not. It's just that it's not right for our streets." In the books they had other trails which they laid, like making marks on trees and leaving arrows made of twigs, but that would not work either. Then I had a brainwave.

"Who's in charge of the chalk in school?"

This time nothing could go wrong. The hares set off, chalking arrows on walls and doubling over in the middle of a quick run to mark one on the pavement, causing no end of obstruction to innocent pedestrians who only saw flying pigtails, a flurry of dresses and a huge chalked arrow, and wondered where the fire was. The game was a complete success.

One day, however, I decided that there must be more to literature than posh schoolgirl stories. I wandered along the aisles, starting right at the beginning and working through the alphabet. I came to M and fixed on Ethel Mannin. Her *Late Have I Loved Thee* gave me no end of problems. She continually referred to *The Confessions of St Augustine*, but St Augustine was a stranger to me. I searched under A again, but Augustine's *Confessions* were not to be found. I plucked up courage and approached Tim.

"Could you get me *The Confessions of St Augustine*, please?"

"The what?"

"*The Confessions of St Augustine*; the book is not on the shelves."

"To be sure it's not," he said. "What do ye want it for?" It wasn't every day in the week that Tim was asked by a twelve-year-old for such a ponderous title and he was entitled to be suspicious.

"This book," and I produced Ethel Mannin, "keeps referring to St Augustine, and I'd like to see what the author is talking about." He took the book and looked at it.

"I don't have time now," he said. "I'm busy. But I'll look for it when I have a chance." True to his word he did, and on my next visit he had a copy waiting for me, but not to take out. The book belonged to the adult library.

"Take it down to the table and look at it," he said, his booming voice breaking the silence and causing everybody to stare. I felt important with this weighty volume under my arm, but *The Confessions of St Augustine* turned out to be most disappointing and uninteresting, and I didn't understand any of it.

"Well," the librarian said when I handed it back, "were you able to follow it?"

"No," I said.

"I didn't think you would be," he said. "Try something else."

Each week I toured the shelves, picking and choosing, trying out books of all kinds. We had to walk two miles to the library to get our precious fiction book, and two miles back home, so every title had to be given careful consideration before it was brought to the counter to be stamped. This meant reading the opening chapter, skipping through to the middle and sneaking a look at the last page to make sure it had a happy ending. It must have lots of conversation – long chapters without any conversations were sure to be boring. My greatest find was a translation of the Greek legends which brought to life the wonderful adventures of Zeus, Hera, Athena, Aphrodite and Heracles. I didn't understand all of it, though, and began to be afraid that maybe my mother would not approve of what I was reading, so I brought the book back pretty quickly.

The quickest way to the library was up by the canal and around by the grainstore, where if I was lucky there would be a horse and dray waiting to be loaded with grain and I could jump on as it moved away, the driver pretending not to see as I settled myself comfortably, my legs dangling over the back and my library book securely beside me. On the way home, I would settle the shopping bag on my arm, keep a wary eye ahead and, stepping off and on the pavement, I walked home with my eyes glued to the pages. I usually had about a third of my library book read by the time I got there.

When we began to attend the lectures held in the library on winter's evenings, we poked fun at our fears as we headed home through the deserted streets. We walked along by the silent shape of St Catherine's church, the corners of the street dark and forbidding and the gas-lamps flickering uneasily. It was near here that Robert Emmet had been executed.

"Don't look now, you might see him."

"We should carry holy water with us – it wards off all the spirits."

"My father says it's only the ones who are not restin' who suddenly appear to people."

"You've lost me."

"Well Robert Emmet might not be restin' easy. After all, nobody even knows where they buried him."

And with a fearful glance at the grey building we ran, gripping each other's hands, and didn't stop until we could see the lights of Thomas Court Bawn and the public house at the corner of South Earl Street and the twist of the street to Marrowbone Lane and home.

# Breaking the Mould

I T WAS ALMOST a repeat of the day I went into Third Class.
I stood before my mother in the kitchen and nearly
stamped my feet, although I knew she would never toler-
ate that.

"I don't want to go," I said.

"It's a great opportunity, and Mr McCann was good enough
to recommend you." I had been offered a job as a tailor's assistant.

"Why doesn't he get the job for his own daughter then?" I
was tempted to say that she was as thick as two planks and
nobody would offer her a job, but already I was inviting a clip
across the back of the legs.

"She's been fixed up and she's serving in a shop."

"Posh, I suppose," I said with malice. Before my mother
could reply, I announced: "I'm not leaving school. I don't
want to leave school. I like school." And I really did.

I had been given a jolt when some of my friends had not
returned after the summer holidays; they had gone on to sec-
ondary education at private convent schools. That had been
in August, and a whole four months before my fourteenth
birthday, when I would have to face up to leaving school.
Time had been quick in catching up with me.

"You've just turned fourteen years of age; you've gone through eighth class. You have your Primary Certificate," my mother said, "and the nuns can't keep you for ever."

Sadly, I knew this was true. My father's heart condition had invalided him, and further schooling at a fee-paying convent was out of the question.

"I could stay on for another year in eighth class and do the preparatory college scholarship examination," I said hopefully, but less confidently now.

"Again?"

"I came very high up the last time." Had I passed, the preparatory college scholarship would have secured me a place in a boarding school run by the Sisters of Mercy to prepare me for teacher-training. I had not seriously considered becoming a teacher when I sat the exam previously, but anything was better than the prospect now held out to me of becoming a tailor's assistant – not even a tailor's apprentice, because I was a girl. My prized Primary Certificate and my glowing reference from Sister Magdalen at the end of my ten years would gather dust at home, while I swept floors, made appointments and sorted buttons in a pokey little tailor's shop.

"You don't want to work in a factory, do you?" My mother was anxious that none of us would.

Many of my school companions had already gone to the biscuit, tobacco and sewing factories, where their parents or other relatives who worked there had "put in a word" for them. Others were apprenticed as milliners or dressmakers, and some, like Madge, were lucky enough to be apprenticed as sales-ladies in drapery shops. Most of my friends looked forward to leaving school and earning a wage packet.

"No. I just want to stay in school."

"All right. I've thought of that," my mother said, "and after

Christmas I'll enrol you in Skerries College and you can work for the Civil Service examinations. The fees are not too bad – we'll manage them out of your wages."

This was a whole lot better than nothing. I knew my mother was concerned and anxious to do her best for me, whatever it might cost, and the prospect of studying at night-classes gave me something to look forward to. And so, at the age of fourteen, I left school for the last time and went to work for a living.

The day stretched interminably in the two little rooms of the shop. When I wasn't sweeping and dusting, I stood importantly beside the tailor as he measured a client and wrote waist, height and hip measurements into a little book. I tried to put the patterns, which were cut out in cardboard and pinned all over the place, in some sort of order, but when he was in a hurry the tailor scattered them again like Billy be damned. I arranged appointments when people called; there was no telephone in the shop. Just one public phone served the whole area, and woe betide any youngster caught trick-acting in that phone-box – the door would be yanked open and his excuse for being in there would have to be a good one.

My tailor had a good reputation in the trade, and on days when things went well I basked in his reflected glory. He had a workshop at the end of the field behind the shop, where he employed three tailors, each an expert in his own line. They collected their work from the shop in the morning, but during the day I was dispatched with linings or sleeves, or pants with "take-in" or "let-out" marks and mysterious V's, dotted and slatted lines, which they understood perfectly and pretended not to, as they muttered and unpicked and tacked. One man was expert in the way a sleeve should sit on a jacket and how to unroll the swell of the cloth across the underside

of a collar; another specialised in pants-making and could reg-
ulate to the barest fraction of an inch where the pants should
break above the shoe; there was one who did the unpicking
and the tacking and the canvas linings and knew how much
wadding should be placed across the shoulders and exactly
where. Cutting the patterns for gents and ladies suits and
overcoats was the prime responsibility of the tailor himself.
Cloth was scarce, and people juggled their clothing coupons
to buy serge and tweed for suits that were expected to last for
twenty years, or till the war was over at least.

The tailor's customers came from far and near, and I worried about the lies I had to tell them when their order was not
quite ready for fitting, until one day a gentle parish priest
from Clondalkin, sensing my distress as I made some feeble
excuse for my boss's absence, calmly said to me:

"I know you're telling me a lie, child, but it's not really a lie.
I know he's not out, but he's out to me and other customers
like me, when he's not ready to see us. But that's what we call
a professional lie, a business lie, child, and you're not to worry
about it."

In early May, after just six months in the shop, my chance
came. My feet hardly touched the ground as I raced down the
Back of the Pipes for home. Folding through the *Evening
Herald* as I tidied up, I spotted an advertisement for "Irish
Proficiency Scholarship Examinations" in the Technical
School on the Rathmines Road. I was within the age group.

"Can I enter?" Breathlessly I held the paper out to my
mother.

She read the advertisement slowly. "I don't know," she said.
I sensed a note of hesitancy in her voice: she had not said
"no".

"We could save the money we spend on Skerries College," I
said. I had been attending classes there on Monday evenings

and I was not liking it one little bit. I had already crossed swords with the Irish teacher. Determined to get value for the fees we were paying, I had shot up my hand after the second lesson and in full voice told him and the class that I could speak Irish fluently, having spent a month in the Connemara Gaeltacht, but had not yet mastered Irish grammar. So could we start with the basics? I enquired. He had closed the roll book with a smart slap and fixed me with a steely gaze.

"I was not engaged to teach students the rudiments of our native language," he said scathingly, "and you're not expected to understand Irish grammar. Just learn it off by heart like everybody else. How many more of you are beginners?" he shouted, but not one hand was raised to accompany mine. After this incident he left me severely alone.

Now my mother weighed this new prospect. "We'll wait till the others come home," she said, "and see what they say."

"Let me sit the examination anyway, please?" I pleaded when Madge and Babs came home from work. This opportunity had not been there for them; Babs was herself working hard to prepare for the Civil Service examinations.

I sat the examination and won a scholarship, which gave me a whole two years of free education in general and secretarial subjects. A new life was opening up for me, and once the scholarship was confirmed there was no doubt in anybody's mind but that I should avail of it. That it should be rejected because I would not pull my weight, and because the family would be without my earnings for two years, never entered their heads. My mother's concern now was to make sure that I would be properly clothed and shod for the walk to and from Rathmines. Most assuredly there would be few pennies for buses.

Jennie's parents decided that she should join me on the two-year secretarial course, and we covered the two-and-a-half miles there and back each day. As well as learning practical skills in typewriting, shorthand and commerce, new doors in literature were opened for me by the college's understanding English teacher. Our circle of friends widened as we joined the choral group, took drama lessons and went to gymnastics classes. Jennie was with me on the day we went to Radio Eireann's studio in Henry Street to record with our choir, which had won an inter-schools choral competition. In our navy gymslips and white blouses, we filed demurely up the long stairs, but with the recording over the heady air of success went to our heads, and we slid down the polished bannisters and scampered out to the street before the astonished porter had a chance to open his mouth.

I lived for the Friday night drama group. I would leave school at five o'clock and walk home; my mother would have tea ready on the table and I would walk back again to Rathmines for practise at seven o'clock. I still had stars in my eyes, and dreamed of being discovered by a scout from the Abbey Theatre. Yet I could not afford to lose sight of the reason I was at vocational school. At the end of the two-year course, the school would place us in clerical work according to our standard and ability.

As these carefree days were drawing to a close, I spent one glorious month in the Rannafast Gaeltacht in Donegal with new friends, Clare, Betty, Vera and Kathleen. We shared Máiréad Rua's house with four girls from Belfast. During the day we wandered the boreens and at night sat beside the turf fire listening to the rapid flow of the old people's conversation, and the *seanchaí* telling stories in the bright, clipped dialect of Donegal. One long evening as we watched the sun melt into the horizon beyond Tory island, we vowed eternal friendship, and I felt my friends' support like arms stretched about me. As we gazed at the clouds tinged with red and purple and gold, I knew they sensed my sadness. My father had died just four weeks before.

I looked out over the Atlantic, remembering other water and another day. So clearly it came to me. I had been nine years old when one of the most severe winters we ever had hit the country. Black frost defied a wintry sun and kept the temperature below freezing. When my father heard that the pond in the Phoenix Park was frozen, he took Madge, Babs, Betty and me to the vast new skating-rink. We slithered on our gaitered feet to the edge of this wonderful icy world and then, taking one of us girls in each hand, he led us over the ice in the safety of his firm grip.

My father had always been there for us, his arms around us in any childish crisis, helping and encouraging and so proud of our smallest achievement. We must go now and progress without him. I missed him, and yearned to hear the voice which said, one day as we were counted through the railway stile at Sandymount:

"Every one of them is mine, Sir. And the other half-dozen, well I left them behind."

The world of business was beckoning. My friends and I were looking forward to a life where we would be part of an army of office workers. We would wear navy office-coats and fiddle with complicated switchboards. We would experience the waxy smell of Gestetner stencils and oozing black ink, and jam earphones on our heads to listen to wax cylinders churning out crackly dictation. I took my first office job at sixteen and I did not shy away this time. It was a new world awaiting me, a world of new possibilities and opportunities – and of risks to my immortal soul, according to my mother. She insisted that I join Madge and Babs and become a Child of Mary, and attend the monthly Sodality meetings which were held in the convent at the unsociable hour of seven o'clock on a Sunday evening. I felt that socials and *céilídhe* were beckoning and I needed nylon stockings, which I could purchase for half the weekly pocket-money my mother allowed me from my wages, the princely sum of two shillings and sixpence.

"Where's Jennie?" Betty asked one evening as we were about to make a trip into town to look at the fashions.

"I don't know," I said; "she's hard to get these days. There's some mystery going on."

When we next came together at our favourite talking place – my mother's front gate – Jennie let us in on her secret. "I'm entering the Carmelite Convent," she said in a quiet little voice.

I whirled the gate shut and goggled at her as she stood, hesitant, before me.

"You're what?" I yelped.

"I'm going to be a nun."

"You can't be. They won't take you. You have to be eighteen."

"I'll be eighteen shortly," Jennie said, "and I'll enter then."

"So that's what all the mystery was about. You never told me," I said accusingly, "and I'm your best friend."

"I couldn't," Jennie said. "I had to be sure first that they'd take me. Don't spread it around too much," she pleaded.

I kept my part of the bargain, but the news still spread like wildfire. This was a neighbour's child, and the whole road basked in the honour. A child for the religious life: suddenly Jennie was important. People knocked at her parents' door to ask what she would need to take with her to the convent and to offer presents, and a collection was taken up to mark this wonderful occasion with a presentation.

All too soon the day dawned for Jennie's entry to the enclosed order of Carmelites. I found it hard to understand what she was doing, and had tried to persuade her to consider a teaching or mission order, but her mind was made up.

"We'll never see you again!"

"Of course you will," Jennie answered. "Well, you will some time. I'm not sure when..."

Betty and I shirked the final parting; we said our goodbyes privately and awkwardly. We were nowhere to be seen when Jennie called to say goodbye to my mother, and neither were we around to smile sadly in the final photographs.

When we did venture near her convent, her voice came to us from behind a curtained grille and frightened the wits out of us. But Jennie had not changed; if anything, her life as a novice made her bubble with freshness and laughter. In my heart I knew it took courage to do what she had done. Jennie had chosen the better part.

By now the war in Europe had drawn to its weary close. I was working with J.C. Parkes & Son on the Coombe, a Catholic rubbing shoulders with a predominantly Protestant workforce, and I considered I had good prospects before me. My journey each day to work brought me past the humpty-dumpty houses along the Coombe, and I watched humpty-dumpty women trailing babies in through the open gates of the Coombe Lying-in Hospital. I began to wonder at their swollen bodies and at a life to which I had not yet given much thought. The path to marriage and motherhood lay open to me. I had, I felt, travelled down some roads, and I looked forward to travelling some more.